From Courbet to Cézanne
A new 19th Century

Preview of the Musée d'Orsay, Paris

From Courbet to Cézanne
A new 19th Century

Preview of the Musée d'Orsay, Paris

The Brooklyn Museum
March 13 - May 5, 1986

Dallas Museum of Art
June 1 - August 3, 1986

Editions de la Réunion des musées nationaux

Front cover : Pierre Bonnard, *La partie de croquet,* detail

ISBN : 2-7118-2.043-2

This exhibition was organized by the Musée d'Orsay,
the Dallas Museum of Art and the Brooklyn Museum,
with the cooperation of the Réunion des musées nationaux.

This exhibition was made possible by a generous grant
from American Airlines, Inc., which is also its official carrier.

An indemnity has been provided by the Federal Council
on the Arts and Humanities, Washington, D.C.

Exhibition organizers :

Michel Laclotte
Inspecteur général des musées, chargé des collections du Musée d'Orsay, Paris

Guy Cogeval
Conservateur stagiaire au Musée d'Orsay, Paris

Caroline Mathieu
Conservateur au Musée d'Orsay, Paris

Steven A. Nash
Deputy Director and Chief Curator, Dallas Museum of Art

Author of the catalog :

Guy Cogeval

Translation by :
Domingo Barbiery
James Mayor

Acknowledgements of the author

I would like, first of all, to thank Léone Nora, in charge of Public Relations at the Musée d'Orsay, whose energy, patience and tenacity have made this exhibition possible.

I am also extremely grateful to Sophie Hanappier for her irreplaceable assistance, and to Anne Roquebert for her continually precious advice.

My entire admiration is reserved for Richard C. Willett, whose vast culture permitted to iron out numerous difficulties in the translation.

My warmest thanks to the following for their contribution in the elaboration and the realization of this project:

Luce Abélès, Eve Alonso, William Arthur, Roseline Bacou, Françoise Baron, Marc Bascou, Béatrice Berthier, Irène Bizot, Marie-Louise Bossuat, Alexis Brandt, Geneviève Bresc, Yvonne Brunhamer, Françoise Cachin, Isabelle Cahn, Marie-Sophie Clémot, Ute Collinet, Jean Coudane, Marie-Laure Crosnier-Leconte, Liliane Degrace, Anne Distel, Anne Dumas, Bruno Dury, Claire Frèches, Françoise Fur, Jean-René Gaborit, Sylvie Gache-Patin, Sophie Guillot, Christel Haffner, Antoinette Hallé, Françoise Heilbrun, Jacqueline Henry, Martine Kahane, Clio Karageorghis, Virginie Herbin, Geneviève Lacambre, Monique Laurent, Marie-Agnès Le Bayon, Brigitte Legars, Antoinette Le Normand-Romain, François Lesure, Catherine Lévy-Lambert, Henry Loyrette, Laure de Margerie, Chantal Martinet, Régis Michel, Philippe Néagu, Emmanuelle Pain, Bruno Pfäffli, Jim Purcell, Debrah Richards, Michèle Rongus, Pierre Rosenberg, Elisabeth Salvan, Roland Schaer, Arlette Sérullaz, Philippe Thiébaut, Bernard Toulet, Jeanne Veyrin-Forrer, Nicole Wild, Christophe Zagrodski, Michèle Marsol.

If the visitors have derived some pleasure from this exhibition, it is also due to the generosity of the following institutions and of the curators who have permitted to enlarge this rapid survey of the nineteenth century's second half:

Musée du Louvre
Département des Peintures
Cabinet des Dessins
Département des Sculptures

Bibliothèque nationale
Département de la Musique
Bibliothèque de l'Opéra
Département des Imprimés
Réserve des Livres précieux
Bibliothèque de l'Arsenal

Musée de la Publicité

Musée Rodin

Musée national de Céramique de Sèvres

Exhibition sponsored by

American Airlines, Inc.

Contents

Foreword

Steven A. Nash

Deputy Director and Chief Curator
Dallas Museum of Art

Upon opening its doors in Paris in December 1986, the new Musée d'Orsay will immediately become one of the greatest art museums in the world. Conceived as the central national museum in France for art produced between 1848 and 1914, it will consolidate under one roof diverse collections of paintings, drawings, and sculpture, including many of the most renowned and beloved masterworks from the Impressionist and Post-Impressionist eras. To create a fuller picture of social and artistic context, however, and justly represent the wide diversities of the period, collections of posters, prints, photography, architectural materials, and decorative arts will also be included. Thus, we can look forward to the most complete survey ever assembled of 19th century art and life in all its complexity and fecundity. As is only appropriate, the physical setting for the new museum is also an exciting work of art. With its steel and glass superstructure and Beaux-Arts facade, the Gare d'Orsay was originally one of Paris' busiest and most elaborate railroad stations, standing along the Seine as a symbol of the dual ambitions of industrial progress and Belle Epoque luxury. It is now being carefully restored and equipped with modern climate control and a new inner structure of galleries and public spaces. The building itself will be a strong attraction once the collection is open.

Given the enormity of achievement that the new Musée d'Orsay represents, it is particularly auspicious and exciting to be able to present in Dallas and Brooklyn a preview of its offerings. Much more than just a selection of favorite works, this exhibition has been carefully conceived and chosen around certain central themes — avant-garde vs. Salon, political observation, Japonisme, etc. — to give it intellectual structure as well as visual appeal. Those of us on the staffs of the Dallas Museum of Art and The Brooklyn Museum are much indebted to our French colleagues for making the exhibition possible. We particularly wish to recognize Jacques Rigaud, President de l'établissement public du musée d'Orsay, and Michel Laclotte, director of the Orsay project, for their dedication to the concept of an exhibition, and Guy Cogeval, Caroline Mathieu, and Léone Nora, for the efforts and knowledge they devoted to its realization. Robert Buck and Sarah Faunce, respectively the Director and the Chairman of Paintings and Sculpture at The Brooklyn Museum, and Harry Parker, Director of the Dallas Museum of Art, have also supported the project from its inception.

Special acknowledgement must also go to American Airlines. Were it not for their generous support, the exhibition could not have taken place. Indeed, discussions between representatives of the Dallas Museum and the French Ministry of Culture about the possibilities of such a project first took place during a trade mission to France sponsored by American Airlines at the time of inauguration of its service to Paris in April 1985.

All of us who have worked on this exhibition are proud to be a part of so important an example of international museum cooperation. It represents yet another step in the sharing and propagation of our respective national heritages.

Preface

Jacques Rigaud

Président de l'Etablissement Public
du Musée d'Orsay

This year, the Orsay Museum will open its doors to the public just before Christmas.

Between the moment when the idea of housing the national collection of art from the second half of the 19th century in a former train station was conceived by those directing the Museums of France and the moment when it will welcome its first visitor, more than 12 years of efforts will have passed with the unyielding perserverance of the last three French Presidents : Georges Pompidou who approved the principle, Valéry Giscard d'Estaing who undertook the enterprise, and François Mitterrand who confirmed and expanded the project, bringing it to fruition.

Throughout the years and especially since work got underway in 1980, numerous American friends and visitors have met with the staff of the museum. Architects, decorators, curators, art historians, journalists, collectors, artists, urban planners, engineers, public officials from every walk of life and from every State of the Union have passed through the museum's doors. Their visit often concluded with the same remark, " What you're doing here really fascinates us. You've got to exhibit and explain your project in the States. "

It is not an easy task that we have undertaken and we are eager to share our attachment to the Orsay Station and Hotel, magnificent examples of late 19th century iron architecture, as well as to convey the extreme complexity of its restoration and the uses to which it will be put. We would like to present a small echo of the richness of its collections and the diversity of the currents and tendancies represented therein. This is done not by an arbitrary choice of selected masterpieces, but by covering the epoch through the themes which touched upon all the techniques of creation — painting, sculpture, architecture, drawing, art objects, music, literature, photography, and cinema. Also represented are the tendancies of this abundant period — Eclectism, Realism, Symbolism, Natural-ism, Impressionism, the Nabi painters, the birth of the Fauve movement, and decorators faithful to the Second Empire decor along with the supporters of Art Nouveau.

We hope this exhibition will lead the spectator onto new pathways of his own imagination and that he will have the chance to visit our own museum in Paris next year !

We would like to thank our partner American Airlines for its generosity and the management of the museums of Dallas and Brooklyn for their enthusiasm. Our most sincere wish is that their endeavors be crowned by the success of this exhibition.

1. An aerial view of the Musée d'Orsay

Le musée d'Orsay

Michel Laclotte

Inspecteur général des musées,
chargé des
Collections du musée d'Orsay

Is it really necessary to set up another museum in a city which already contains so many ? What will the public be able to see there ? In answering these questions, it may be possible to arouse the curiosity of its future visitors.

Anyone who has visited the Jeu de Paume these past few years has noticed the crampedness and discomfort of the place. In 1947 when it first opened to display the Impressionist paintings, it was an ideal setting surrounded by the luminous open spaces of the Tuileries Gardens. Unfortunately, thirty years later, the museum could no longer present its collection with dignity. The size of the collection had grown considerably, enriched by gifts and purchases. The public too was growing, drawn to Impressionism by its universal attraction, and could no longer be accomodated without risk.

The expansion of the museum was even more necessary after the transfer of the National Museum of Modern Art in 1977 from its former site (The Palais de Tokyo) to its new one at the Georges Pompidou Center. This offered a chance for a new and massive enlargement of the collection. The Post-Impressionist paintings (the Pont Aven school, Neo-Impressionism) and a large number of works by French and foreign artists, coming out of Naturalism and Symbolism at the end of the 19th century, which had belonged to the National Museum of Modern Art (itself heir to the former Museum of Luxembourg), were transferred to the Louvre. From that time on, works that historians could no longer continue to group with " modern art " were transferred from one museum to another on a periodical basis. Temporarily displayed at the Palais de Tokyo (from 1978) under the heading of Post-Impressionism, these works (painting, sculpture, objets d'art) were certainly destined one day to join the works of the Impressionists. Signac and Cross were to encounter Seurat as Emile Bernard and Sérusier meet up with their friend Gauguin.

Even expanding the Jeu de Paume facilities wouldn't have been enough to absorb the growth of its collection, especially taking into account one of those phenomena of resurgence upon which Art History and taste thrive : the rediscovery of a " new " 19th century, much less linear and concise that the one which the preceeding critics had described in their manner of seeing everything as either all good or all bad.

Since the memorable exhibition " Sources of the 20th century " (Paris, 1960) which definitely placed Art Nouveau among the great movements which one after the other completely jolted and enriched Western Art, a good deal of other resurrections have followed : those of Symbolism, industrial architecture, the " Beaux Arts " style of architecture, the eclectism of the Second Empire, photography, and different schools of American and European painting which until a certain time had been eclipsed outside of their national boundaries by the sunlight of Parisian painters.

In more than one case this realignment of values remains debatable or unfinished. It is undeniable that it ignites, as with every flare up of fashion, the questionable enthusiasm of snobbery and speculation ; not every artist in the process of re-evaluation is a scandalously forgotten genius. However, through books, articles and exhibitions a new vision of the 19th century has been developing for the last 20 years, a vision that an improved Jeu de Paume museum could never have developed on its own.

For such a display, space was needed, and plenty of it. This became available in the Gare d'Orsay, a closed down train station on the other side of the Seine facing the Louvre and the Tuileries.

The hopes and proposals of the Direction of French Museums were answered in 1973, under the government of Georges Pompidou, when it was decided that this train station would house all of the arts from the second half of the 19th century. Threatened with demolition (plans had been drawn up to build a huge hotel on the spot), the station, whose railway activity had been reduced to commuter trains, was saved. The building, long considered a monstrosity of bad taste, benefitted from the renewed interest for the 19th century (the Halles market place, destroyed in 1971-72, had not been able to take advantage of this historical stroke of luck). After an interval during which effort was basically going into the construction of the Georges Pompidou Center, the project was conclusively undertaken and supported by M. Giscard d'Estaing. In 1978 a public board was created to follow through with the operation. François Mitterrand in 1981 confirmed the importance of the project. In this way three presidents of the French Republic guaranteed the continuity of a difficult and necessary enterprise — the creation of a new museum.

The novelty of the museum lies not only in its program in so far as its *contents* : the collections, that which is displayed before the public. It also lies in its *containing* : the building itself embodies the adaptation of an old train station-hotel to a new use as a multidisciplinary museum.

To say a few words about the *contents,* as a national museum, the Orsay Museum stores the state collections illustrating art from the second half of the 19th century and the first few years of the 20th century. It is set between the Louvre museum which holds the national collection of works before 1850 and the National Museum of Modern Art entrusted with works dating after the period of 1905-1910 (with a few exceptions for artists born before 1870).

A great deal of consideration and debate went into the discussions leading to the dates limiting the collection, beginning with 1848-1850, and ending with 1905-1910. At first it was suggested that the beginning date extend as far back as the Romantic period, but that would have entailed an even larger museum. It was then moved forward to 1863, a date which is relevant only for French painting. Finally it was decided that the middle point of the century corresponded with a change in every area, not just in the political and social spheres : the emergence of Courbet and Millet in the Salons of 1849 and 1850, the foundation of the Preraphaelite Brotherhood in 1848, the construction of Paxton's Crystal Palace (1850-1851), and that of the new wing of the Louvre (dating from 1852) were among the signs of new developments which were to encorporate, at the other end of the chain, their own rupture with Picasso's Demoiselles d'Avignon (1907).

2. A view of Montmartre from one of the Orsay clock towers

3. The façade of the old station

Covering a considerably dense and prolific period, the museum's ambition is to evoke its diversity completely by demonstrating the artistic creativity expressed not only in painting, sculpture, decorative and graphic arts but also in other visual arts such as architecture, urbanism and cinema. Other means of circulating images will also be presented (i.e. the poster, the illustrated book and the press). There will be small exhibits of thematic "documents", films and various audio-visual devices which will permit the visitor to discover the ties and correlations that link the visual arts and other artistic media of the time (literature, and of course music for which there will be regularly scheduled concerts). All of these elements will be presented in a historical framework.

Through its interdisciplinary program, the Orsay museum will be able to distinguish itself from the Louvre and Modern Art museums in Paris.

For its ambitious plans to be put into action and for all the creative styles of the period to be represented, the initial contributions (painting, sculpture and very rare objets d'art dispersed between the Louvre, the Jeu de Paume and the Palais de Tokyo) were evidently not enough. These ambitions became realities through the aid of other museums or administrations (Versailles, Fontainebleau, Compiègne, the Museum of Decorative Arts, the Mobilier National and the Sèvres Porcelaine Manufacture) who consented to entrust important pieces to the Orsay Collection. By offering other works in compensation, we were able to bring back paintings and sculptures, property of the State that had been sent to museums in the provinces. Above all a veritable policy of acquisition was pursued. The museum benefitted from the generosity of numerous donators among whom were the recent Friends of the Museum Society, from the gratuity of certain major works offered in lieu of state taxes, and finally by active campaigns of purchasing, promoted by special credit funds. Of course this meant that gaps could be filled in the existing collections while others could be set up in their entirety, practically starting from scratch. This was the case for the objets d'art and furnishings, architecture and photography. On the other hand, instead of creating new archives of engravings or printed material, we decided to call regularly upon the Bibliothèque Nationale (National Library) to present those diverse techniques (including posters and illustrated books).

To name a few statistics, not counting the works on loan that are returning from the provinces, since 1978 the museum has acquired in both purchases and gifts 270 paintings, 280 sculptures, 550 objets d'art, over a thousand photographs, and various pieces concerning architecture. Even with all of these acquisitions, it will still be difficult to say that the museum offers a truly complete panorama of art from the second half of the 19th century. Great artists, particularly painters foreign to France are still wanting. Certain movements, schools and techniques are either not represented or insufficiently so. Our aim has been to attempt to demonstrate, as broadly as possible, the creative abundance along with the advantageous contradictions which characterized the period while trying not to create any artificial equilibrium between the movements. If the museum reflects the opportunities of the art market, the predilections of the connoisseurs the generosity of a family who helped to place a certain artist in the museum who might merit less esteem than another, so much the better. A museum cannot give an impersonal and strictly objective lesson like an encyclopedia. It can only reflect the tastes or rather the choices, the refusals and omissions of collectors, curators and patrons of the arts who have from one generation to another built up its collections.

Let us wager that the future will complete, retouch, and debate the image of the 19th century which the Orsay museum offers today.

As for the act of *containing,* the building that is destined to house the collections, the Orsay Station and Hotel were constructed by Victor Laloux at the former site of the Cour des Comptes devastated by fire in 1871. Built in less than two years, the edifice was inaugurated on July 14th 1900, at the height of the World Fair. At the peak of its activity, under its monumental vaults it bore witness to the bustle of ticket counters, waiting rooms and the baggage depot, while the trains ran underneath the building. The four hundred rooms and reception halls of the deluxe hotel enclosed the station on two sides. Pompously hiding the metallic structures, the freestone façades rivalled the other palaces on the banks of the Seine.

This railroad monster was now to be converted to its new function as an art museum. Space had to be devised and designated to exhibit both the permanent presentation of the works and temporary exhibitions. There had to be rooms for reception, storage, workshops, studios and other various services. The best lighting for each exhibit with suitable itineraries for the public had to be assured. All this was to be embarked upon while preserving the identity of Laloux's building.

An answer to these needs was furnished by the laureate architects of the 1979 competition (R. Bardon, P. Colboc, J.P. Philippon) and the Italian architect Gae Aulenti, laureate of a second consultation for interior architecture and research into museum lay-out. The nave has received a new construction, enhancing the vaulted ceiling under which an axial court opens up crossing the grand hall from east to west, in the direction of the former tracks. The museum rooms are surmounted with terraced roofs ; these communicate with galleries arranged on two levels continuing from halls that run the length of the nave and overlook the Seine. At the top of the building under the immense roof, spacious galleries make optimum use of the natural lighting from above. The heavily decorated hotel reception halls on the second floor are integrated into the museum circuit with the restaurant which will now serve museum visitors rather than hotel guests. The three principal exhibit levels are joined together by intermediary staircases and escalators at the two ends of the gallery.

The challenge for the architects was their refusal to do any stylistic imitation, or form any links between the old train station and the new museum which was to replace it. The iron beams and pillars of the original Laloux construction (including the invisible elements of the station, the roof and pavilions) and its

4. The dining-room
of the former Hôtel d'Orsay
which will become
the restaurant of the museum

22

stucco decor have been preserved, restored and accentuated. The new structures, as sturdy as they can be in their stone dressing and their metallic geometry, leave throughout the perceptible presence of the original edifice.

Unified by the materials and colors used to decorate the inside (stone from Burgundy, light-colored partitions, dark brown or blue metals, for example) the interior architecture arranges a succession of distinctly diversified rooms, each conceived with concern for the works presented and demonstrating numerous architectural solutions to the problems posed by creating such environments.

The challenge, once accepted, became wedded to the museographic program in all of its richness and complexity. To avoid clutter and confusion the planners chose to split up and diversify the itinerary. It was first necessary to distinctly separate the didactic zones (thematic exhibitions, consultation areas, audio-visual events) from those consecrated only to the art pieces necessitating visual serenity and tranquility. The often unavoidable distinctions between different modes of expression and different techniques had to be taken note of, keeping away from gratifying associations which artificially aim at restoring the " atmosphere " of an era even at the price of historical truth. By linking certain ideas on the visitor's itinerary, we have hoped to bring out the tensions and antagonisms between esthetically opposed tendancies of the time ; for instance, presenting two distinct zones, on one hand the development of Impressionism (after 1870) followed by Post-Impressionism, and on the other hand the contemporary pictorial trends which were blindly confused in a same aversion by 20th century critics who grouped everything together under the label of *Pompiers*

The presentation of the collection is thus unfurled through the three levels, through a pattern of " sequences " each clearly differentiated from the other by their contents and by the architectural setting which has been chosen as characteristic.

The first level is consacrated to the period from 1848 to 1875. It is entered into after a historic introduction (showing films and objects in " flashes " illuminating the historical and sociological make up of the second half of the 19th century). Continuing along the first level, each side of the great hall is allotted to sculpture from Rude to Carpeaux in two long parallel sections. On one side we find works stemming from the Realist period to the beginning of Impressionism ; one the other, the heritage of the Romantics (Delacroix) and of the Neo-Classicists (Ingres) who engendered eclecticism and Symbolism. Eclecticism dominates the decorative arts rooms and triumphs in the Opera room which honors both the achievement of Garnier and the performances given therein. On the same level, space is devoted to a rotating exhibit of drawings, engraving and photography as well as thematic exhibitions concerning the period 1848-1875.

To reach the second level at the top of the building, one can take the escalators installed at the far end of the great hall, near the various rooms of the Pavilion dedicated to temporary and permanent presentations concerning architecture and urbanism. The second level itself is the longest of the museum, that devoted to

Impressionism after 1870 and the diverse reactions that it provoked (Neo-Impressionism, the Pont-Aven school, the Nabis). A coffee shop and an audiovisual consultation zone can be found in addition to exhibits dedicated to the graphic arts.

The descent towards the third level of the visit on the second floor is punctuated by displays from the archives on journalism, posters and book illustrations coupled with historical information found in the Gallery of Dates.

The third and final stage of the visit takes place in the former reception hall of the hotel which reveals the art and official decorating style of the Third Republic. There, the museum-goer can rediscover the vast spaces of the nave and the terraces which overlook the courtyard where sculpture is presented from the last third of the 19th century (dominated by Rodin) up to the beginning of the 20th century (Maillol and Bourdelle). The first group of rooms opening up onto the terraces offers diverse aspects of Naturalism, Symbolism and turn of the century academic art. Afterwards comes a large section of French and Belgian Art Nouveau which leads the visitor up the two towers at the far end of the great hall, one devoted to Guimard, the other to the masters of Glasgow, Vienna and Chicago. After a succession of displays organized for the thematic exhibitions covering the period of 1870 to 1910, a last series of rooms are devoted to the further development of the first Nabi painters after 1900 (Bonnard, Vuillard, Denis) with an introduction to the art of the 20th century, describing the situation in the art world during the period from 1904 to 1906 (Matisse and the Fauves). The visit ends with a last " picture show " — the word being à propos for it concerns the birth of the cinematographic arts.

5. Longitudinal section of the museum
   Original drawing by Gae Aulenti

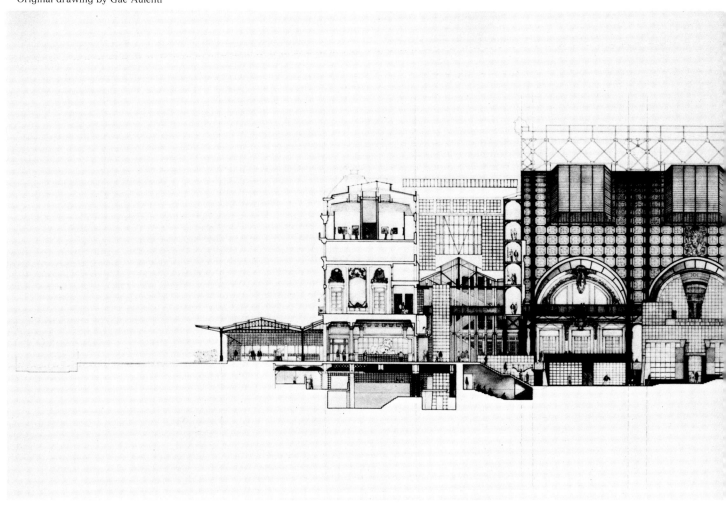

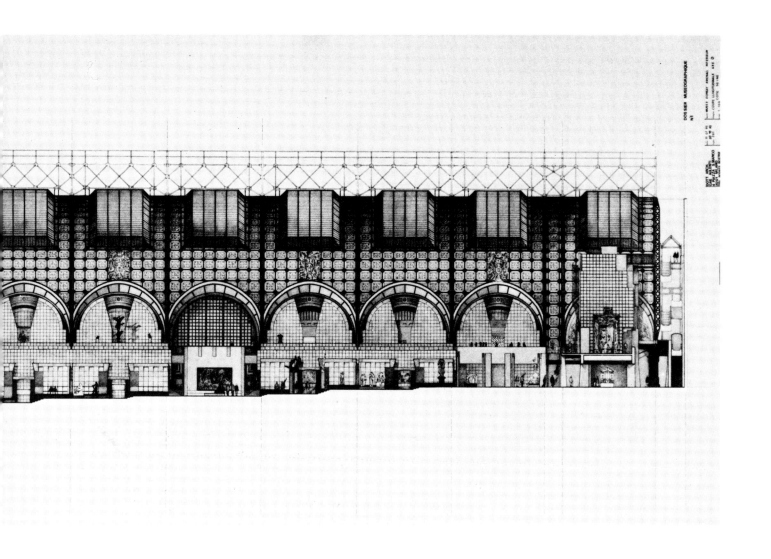

6. Cross section of the museum
Original drawing by Gae Aulenti

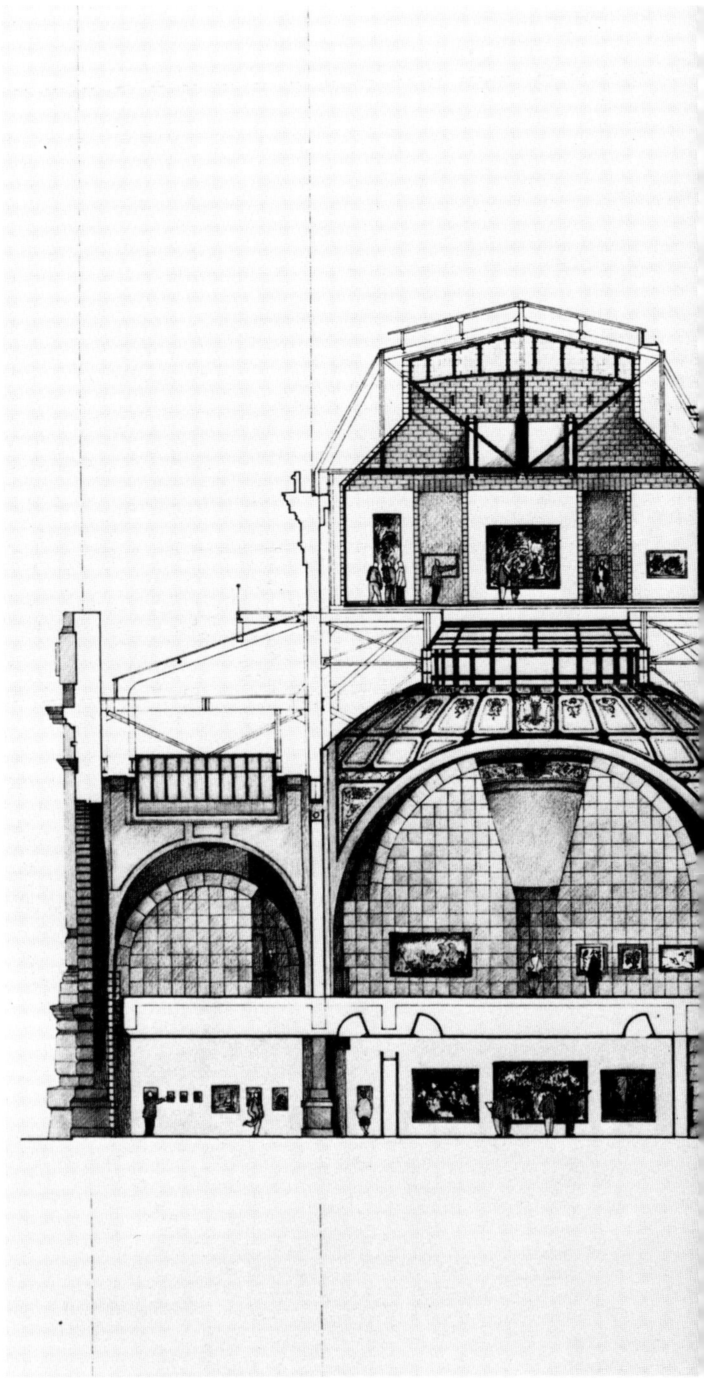

Catalog

The aim of this catalog is not to offer a series of descriptions concerning each and every work of art. The extreme diversity of the collection invalidated this conception proper to exhibitions consacrated to one painter or to a particular artistic tendency. For this edition, we preferred to present a series of themes, segments transversing the twilight of the nineteenth century, blending together the works from the Musée d'Orsay as reference points along the pathway of the commentary : painting, sculpture, objets d'art, drawings and even films.

The chapters do not claim to be exhaustive scientific analysis of each theme, but instead fortuitous opportunities for reflection. The commentary of the works, coming at the end of each chapter in which they are mentioned, gives but few specifications : title, date, dimensions (for the paintings, drawings, etc., in height, and length ; for the sculptures and objets d'art : height, lenght and width ; each measurement is given in centimeters), conditions of acquisition.

The great majority of works are property of the Musée d'Orsay.

The drawings, aquarelles, washes and etchings are on loan from the Cabinet des Dessins du Musée du Louvre ; some sculptures (Cat. nº 18, 41, 42, 72, 96) are from the Département des Sculptures du Musée du Louvre, as well as few paintings (Cat. nº 1, 4, 8, 11, 65, 67, 83) from the Département des Peintures du Musée du Louvre, all these works will nevertheless be on display at the Musée d'Orsay from the day of its opening. In this catalogue, provenance will be indicated just for the posters, books and scenographic models coming from other institutions.

Contrasts

Legray : The Salon, 1852

Ruptures and Continuity

Scandals erupted over the last of Beethoven's quartets in a music world already turbulent. Even those contemporaries who were closest to him felt unprepared to accord recognition to the radically new musical discourses that they found in these works and considered his series of prophetic compositions as either amusement or provocation — pardonable diversions from a genius who had already proved his worth elsewhere. From then on the scandal has never really died down. Rarely has objective progress not encountered steadfast resistance or vindicative condamnation. Critics found Berlioz's *Damnation of Faust* (1846) to contain not one melodious moment, Wagner's *Tannhäuser* (Paris, 1861) was a combination of gratuitous dissonances, Mussorgsky had no idea how to orchestrate his own music, Debussy was flaccid if not spineless and Mahler sounded like a large empty wardrobe.

Each time it appeared as though the innovators had intentionally meant to shock in order to shake up the stable edifice of convention and to challenge the audiences. It seemed as if music had reached the limits of reason, the point of no return, beyond which there would lie only the 'terra-incognita' of chaos. This reaction was not conceivable in the 18th century: the only popular (and performed) music, was the music of the day, which virtually entered into oblivion the following generation. Thus, during a century of scientific progress all art would be obliged to conform to unwritten 'eternal rules.'

Although Flaubert in his work often emphasized the dominant characteristics of his own century — a marked feeling for history — in the particular domaine of the visual arts everything took place as if the contemporary upheavels, the consequences of a new social order, could only be absorbed at the price of a frenzied maintenance of classical-heroic models, which were to survive by reference to the past. Academism, armed with formulas which finally organized themselves into a veritable visual code, became the cultural guarantor of the power of money, dressing it up in luxurious garments that gave it a timeless value.

Fig. 1
Anonymous: A Room in the Luxembourg Museum
(c. 1880)

Inevitably some members of the conservative and progressive ruling classes gave way to merciless warfare. The Impressionist group reflected for example the same relative diversity of social origins (from the modest Pissarro to the wealthy Manet), as the defenders of the Beaux-Arts. One of the best arguments for the maintainance of state awards and scholarships such as the Prix de Rome, was that they gave opportunities to needy young artists of talent. However it is clear that the combat for modernism did not in any way parallel the class struggle.

Contemporary research, inspired by a historiography more responsive to continuity than to breaks in the rhythm of history, draws attention to contacts between stylistically opposed artists : personal friendships such as those between Alfred Stevens and Edouard Manet, Edgar Degas and Léon Gérôme, shared apprenticeships such as those experienced in the studios of Couture and Gleyre, and iconographic convergences, where, to give one example, the work of Alfred Boime is particularly notable.

Nevertheless, it is difficult to understand how one can possibly remain unaware of the breaking point that shook the foundations of the entire period between Courbet and Gauguin, how the prodigious acceleration in the history of forms that proceeded so spontaneously from one movement to the next (Naturalism / Impressionism / Pointillism / Symbolism / Cloisonnism / Fauvism) could have remained hidden from view, and the disintegration of each movement unregarded. As the train of modernism raced forward, the sense of alarm became widespread. The Academy feared confronting its uselessness, institutions trembled from the strain of upholding their self resect, while the average bourgeois believed that he was still being treated with contempt. Oswald Spengler inveighed against decadence and Emile Zola, who had been the first to approve of the movement, proclaimed his horror at its uncontrollable influence.

Of course there is no real 'tabula-rasa' of the Impressionists. Like the Pre-Raphaelites and later the Symbolists, their painting followed a system of

Fig. 2
Daumier: The «Refusés»

Fig. 3
Manet: Portrait of Émile Zola (1868)

Fig. 4
Daumier: The Public at the Salon (1852)

Fig. 5
Manet: The Asparagus (1880)

Fig. 6
Manet: Dead Toreador (1866)

values in which both good and evil were opposed, albeit in an extremely subtle manner. As time passed, none of the innovating ideas escaped from the gradual slide towards formulation, that is to say, the restoration of Academism.

The end of the nineteenth century offers the spectacle of a continual struggle against the established schemata by means of an *empirical investigation* of reality. Monet proclaimed a desire to be reborn blind in order to set himself free from any preconceived visual formulas. In making this statement he agreed with Ruskin, for whom the quest for truth supposed an absolute *naïvety of observation,* a state of mind which united the intuitive comprehension of nature with an inflexible investigation of objective reality typical to that of the modern day scientist. Only science could tear away the veil of illusion and remove the fallacies which surrounded the metaphysical and spiritual superstructures.

" Sincerity " became the war cry, the other spectre that haunted Europe. The word was first uttered by the Naturalists. For them no subject could be contemptible per se. Courbet, on the fringes of automatic writing, boasts of painting an object without knowing what it is, as Claude Lantier, the hero of Zola's novel *L'Œuvre* (1886) claimed that a plain carrot could be revolutionary. Manet's *Asparagus* (1880, *fig. 5*) was not perhaps revolutionary but, isolated in its empty and unstable space, it assuredly communicated the same kind of emotion as that found in his *Dead Toreador* (1866, *fig. 6*) which at first sight seems much more dramatic. The old hierarchy of genre painting disappeared with Manet.

The history of modernism begins at the point where landscape is considered to be a suitable subject for painting by itself, that is with Constable, Corot, Daubigny and Rousseau. Manet meanwhile was the first painter to see his painting as a separate reality, as equally concrete as the real world, a reality that was pitted against him. Up until Courbet, each image had appeared to be faithfully drawn from an accumulation of daily experience to be reborn upon the canvas. With Manet the image aquired an absolute presence and had no significance beyond that visibly expressed on the canvas. He closed the gap between the subject matter and ourselves, with Olympia lying upon her unmade bed and the still-lifes that reveal a secret empathy linking Manet with the haphazard.

It was over Manet that the scandal began. In 1863, the Emperor skoffed at the authority of the official Salon's jury and gave permission to the artists who had been refused to show their works in an adjoining Salon. With Manet were Whistler, Fantin-Latour, Pissarro and Jongkind. But, as though to confound our tendancy to categorize, the list of those officiating at the Salon included artists of such varying colors as Winterhalter, Baudry, Corot, Doré, Puvis de Chavannes, Fromentin and Courbet.

It is all too easy to give credance to the idea that the Impressionists were driven to take action in political opposition to the state aesthetics imposed on them by Napoleon III and Nieuwerkerke, the director of Museums. The reality of the situation was much more complex.

What actually happened was a split between those artists who wanted their works to reflect a static moment in time and those who, alive to the dynamism of the world, used painting to capture the changing sensation of reality. It was not a question of two different schools, but rather two functions of art that were to co-exist through mutual exclusion.

At the same time as Manet the Impressionists established the picturalization of their environment. A decade was necessary for the conventions of lighting to be abandoned, such as the linear outlining of forms, or the hatching of lines to indicate shade : color, which up to now had been mere (and often complacent) filling up of space, dominated their compositions ; brush strokes expressing the medium of oil paint, far from being disapproved of, were accepted as the indispensable marks of a personal calligraphy.

The palette was ruled by brighter and clearer colors than those authorized by tradition (lead white, veronese green, cobalt blue, chrome yellow and green, as well as vermillion) and the habit of working out of doors in direct contact with the subject, possible owing to the recent invention of color in zinc tubes, resulted in the evocation of a sunny Paris opened up by Haussmann's transformations that emphasized the terraces, cafés, and walks, as well as the surrounding countryside already threatened by the railways and industry.

The elaboration of a theme : portrait, landscape, seascape, fugitive notion, or whatever, is still, more than ever, founded upon observation, and the impact of that observation upon the consciousness — that is to say the expression of meaning and not the mere transposition of an image. The spectator looking at the painting becomes an actor in a pictorial event, free to locate his focus somewhere between a far-sighted vision where the objects manifest their illusionary presence, and near the canvas where the same objects lose their clarity.

From now on, any literary pretensions of the image tend to diminish in favor of its purely visual qualities. This is a transition that demonstrates the fundamental contribution made by Impressionism to the history of artistic creation, a contribution that reaches beyond the superficiality of the triumphal announcement of the reign of " pure painting ".

All attempts to link Impressionism with Abstraction are not unjustified, but they present numerous dangers of schematization. The perception of reality and its interpretation still remain the point of departure for all Impressionist painting.

The choice of Impressionist subject matter was still closely tied to the shared memory of academic apprenticeship ; this is perceptible in Monet and even more so in the young Degas.

Their innovations should be related to a moving standard that even the traditionalists found hard to apply. Gérôme thought he was reviving Apelle's charm when he painted *An Idyll, Daphnis and Chloé* (1852, *fig. 7*), as Ary Scheffer and William Bouguereau must have believed that they were restoring Raphael in the most affected of their paintings. Nothing appears more nineteenth century and dated than these works claiming eternal beauty in both their treatment and their inspiration. Hegel predicted an inevitable breakdown in the quality of certain religious paintings : " ...the representation of the Eternal Father, of Christ

Fig. 7
Gérôme: An Idyll, Daphnis and Chloé (1852)

Fig. 8
Bouguereau: Consoling Virgin (1877)

Fig. 9
Cabanel: The Birth of Venus (1862)

Fig. 10
Couture: The Romans of the Decadence (1847)

and of Mary may appear as noble and as perfect as we could want, no longer will they have the power to astound." Yet Bouguereau continued to paint his *Consoling Virgins (fig. 8)* of rancid wax which, Duranty claimed, " invariably looked like nannies in their baths or nuns in charge of the dispensary."

Soon the bourgeois public that " desires to be shown as beautiful and believes that it really is so " (Proudhon) would weary of recognizing themselves disguised in the vulgar and pompous clothes in which they had been painted.

Even the painters who attempted to express the intellectual and philosophical preoccupations of their time through traditional allegory rarely escaped ending up with achievements of labored bufoonery, as in the well-known *Romans of the Decadence* (1847, *fig. 10*) by Thomas Couture, or the complex *Divina Tragedia* (1869) by Paul Chenavard.

Prudent critics like Ernest Chesneau, the Goncourt Brothers (enthusiasts of eighteenth century painting before David) or Eugène Fromentin, a specialist of seventeenth century Dutch painting, reached the point of proposing alternatives to these historical odds and ends mistaken for classical tradition. However clever the arguments may have been, by contenting themselves with the superficial convergences between modern painting and traditional academism, or by insisting upon the plausible setting of scenes to which the painter had to conform, they circumvented the essential... The divergence had become so apparent that it marked the existence of a confrontation between parties engaged in a veritable mutation of visual culture. Painting thus shattered the traditional notion of space at the moment when the rejection of the sancrosanct opposition between art and technique was manifesting itself in the hierarchic divisions between the arts.

Photography permitted the Impressionists to verify the value of the affinity between intuition, observation and skill, but while their technique became hazier as they approached their ultimate goal of rendering the complexity of movement, photography was in the process of evolving towards a clearer and neater image, abandoning its early dependance on the consacrated arts.

Throughout the century, architecture had been looking for a language that would embody the elements produced by the new technology in order to transform them rather than submit itself to them. The materials (iron, cast-iron and glass) were adapted to their new functions and cast aside the copying of past styles with a new order of beauty.

The convergences between old and new profoundly deepened the effects of what was to become a virtual change in society. The weight of the Impressionist detour continued to be incumbent upon the evolution of the visual arts until the beginning of the new century, but its ramifications were as numerous as they were complex. The movements that succeeded one another at an incredible rate, in a short period of only thirty years, derive as much from the Impressionist model as from the justified criticism of its fatal degeneration. No innovation was protected against imitation and standardization — genre painting could easily borrow certain tricks of Impressionism to its advantage, thereby safely stealing the veil of modernism. The protagonists themselves, Monet, Pissarro, Degas and above all Cézanne, who never really belonged to the movement, gradually moved away from Impressionism in different directions after 1880.

The expressive confidence of Impressionism, influenced by positivism, made way for both anxiety and uncertainty. The jump forward accomplished by the faculties of perception was probably acquired at the expense of the imagination. This was the fundamental reproach formulated by Symbolism not only against Realism but also towards Impressionism.

Odilon Redon expressed simply the idealistic aspirations of his generation that was " accustomed to dream " : " I refused to embark upon the Impressionist boat because I found the ceiling too low... Real parasites of the object (the Impressionists) have only cultivated art in the visual field and have somewhat closed it off to all that lies beyond and which could, even by the use of black, humbly render the light of spirituality. By this I mean a radiation which seizes our spirit and escapes any analysis. " The Symbolist movement proved that an art with textual reference could survive Impressionism, by above all being sensitive to the secret affinities which linked the different kinds of expression that were all trying to reach the same ideal.

Monet himself appeared sensitive to the oblique reflections of Symbolism when painting his series of " engulfed " *Cathedrals (fig. 11)* in a manner that recalled Whistler. Paul Gauguin, along with Mallarmé, could have been its long awaited guide. However Gauguin's very personal idealism pushed him towards other shores ; his shadowless images, his colors, extremely hostile to nature, and his harmonies which resulted from strong contrasts express his radical refusal of empirical observation. With him, painting really became an autonomous object, the very condition of existence, not merely its allegorical justification. The object, from the very moment of its perception, evolved towards a synthesis of the diverse stages of life. The Nabi painters inherited from Gauguin the fundamental idea of the unity of creation.

Fig. 11
Monet: The Rouen Cathedral - Harmony in Blue (1894)

In a world other than that of dream and twilight enchantment, Seurat attempted to produce a coherent response to the constant need to give a theoretical basis to what had, up to then, been left to intuition. A reader of the scientists Charles Blanc and Chevreul, he foreshadowed Kandinsky's theory of color in his brief writings. Most importantly, his monumental compositions achieved a synthesis of form by the geometrization of light. In sovereign and contemplative calm, he composed his static objects and human subjects on the canvas, depriving them of any individual expression, by connecting the different planes through a molecular series of dabs condensed into little dots, the " optical mixture " exalting colors and re-establishing the underlying design when seen from afar.

It seems that the new century was inaugurated, under the aegis of a revived unity between the various art movements, favored by Art Nouveau as its magnetic center. The 1900 Paris World Fair ordained its triumph. *Modern Style* in England, *Jugendstil* in Germany and Austria, *Liberty* in Italy, it appeared as the first movement on a European scale and foreshadowed the decline of Paris as the

Fig. 12
Seurat: The Circus (1890)

uncontestable center of artistic creation. The destiny of the XXth century was now carved out as much in Vienna around Klimt, Schiele, Mahler, Schönberg, Berg, Webern, Musil and Freud, as in Munich, the " Athens of Mitteleuropa ", where Kandinsky, De Chirico, Kubin and Richard Strauss undertook their formative years.

Originally announced by the decorative arts, Modern Style rapidly pervaded every domain : painting for instance offered a new and propitious field with its tendency towards the two-dimensional expressed by Gauguin and the Nabis. Art Nouveau perpetuated the Symbolist message by insisting upon the coalescence of architecture, mural painting, and decoration as a global phenomenon, destined to produce a comprehensive effect : the general oscillation of the universe could be expressed through the concatenation of the rhythmic dynamism particular to each art form. Evidently, the pursuit of easy effects, which would sway the public, could easily result in the degeneration of Art Nouveau towards some kind of " noodle style ". But the functional concision and the conceptual austerity of works produced by the Glasgow School of Mackintosh, and the Wiener Werkstätte under Josef Hoffmann, prepared for the future investigations of the Bauhaus as well as those of contemporary design.

This complex dialectic between convergence and ruptures continues to thrive at the end of our own century, and at present, we are experiencing the same anxieties. An attempt to evolve this fundamental ambiguity can be made by a shattered series of rapid allusions, composed of brief spot-lighting of limited areas : the lesson of the masters of the past, the study of the nude, photographic portraitism, Orientalism, landscapes, etc.

Models from the Past : Copy or Echo ?

Fig. 13
Daumier : Monsieur Courbet renders his figures much too vulgar...
(1855)

When Pissarro asked that the museums, " the necropolises of art ", be thrown into the fire, he directly provoked the bourgeois who intended to revive the classical ideal in the contemporary world. He behaved in a similar fashion to Daumier when he caricatured a couple of ugly spectators shocked by the realism in a painting by Courbet (" Monsieur Courbet renders his figures much too vulgar, no one in real life is that ugly ", fig. 13), while Alfred Jarry threatened the trembling share-holders with punishment in The " Chanson du décervelage " (Song of Brainwashing) from his "Ubu Cocu ".

When painting shamelessly produced Olympian Gods as if they were moulded in animal fat, or presented armor-clad versions of French History, mockery remained an efficient weapon. The Impressionists were nevertheless sensitive in varying degrees to the lessons of the past.

It comes as no surprise that " the museum painting " to which the Impressionists referred was not the same as that being idolized by the Academy. They preferred the freedom with masses of color that characterized the Venitian school, rather than the severity of drawing inherited from Raphael, at that time

Fig. 14
Courbet: The Painter's Workshop (1855)

Fig. 15
Manet: Le Déjeuner sur l'herbe (1863)

Fig. 16
Titian: Concert champêtre

asepticised by the interpretation of the Beaux-Arts; the " terribilità " of Michelangelo to the miraculous grace of Leonardo da Vinci; and Delacroix rather than Ingres.

This is noticeable in Degas, in whom an Italian sojourn and apprenticeship had developed a passion for Piero della Francesca and Mantegna, as well as in Seurat, a defender of academic tradition in drawing.

The innovators distinguished themselves from the traditionalists, unlike the characters of Flaubert's *Bouvard and Pécuchet,* by refusing to display reference to the past as proof of their erudition — their vision of the past incited them to transpose solutions in response to the demands of their painting.

Courbet, the black sheep of the Institute, proclaimed that the only possible painting was that which rendered modern life, a reality relieved from the sequels of history. And yet, *The Painter's Workshop* (1855, *fig. 14*) can be interpreted as an allegory where Courbet's own self portrait appears on the face of the Creator in his own reproduced Sixtine Chapel which surrounds the room by a play of infinite reflections that irresistibly recall *Las Meniñas* by Velasquez; the reflection of a painting within the painting evokes the mirrored images so dear to the Flemish. This congregation of references is not an end in itself, nor is it a means of ennobling the painting. It indicates a familiar path in the search for the unknown.

Manet went even further. Reacting against the overpolished style that accompanied the conventional subject, he dismantled the venerated models of the grand masters and elaborated a new language through the articulation of their syntax.

In his *Déjeuner sur l'Herbe* (1863, *fig. 15*), Manet was inspired by an engraved *Judgement of Paris* by Marc Antonio Raimondi according to Raphael. The man lying down in the foreground, leaning on his elbow, is an exact transposition of the fluvial divinities of ancient Roman statuary (The Tiber, The Nile, etc.).

The Italian sculptor Pietro Magni made the same reference to Raimondi in his sculpted tableau commemorating *The Opening of the Suez Canal* (1863, year of Manet's *Déjeuner*). His attempt to celebrate a contemporary subject by having

Fig. 17
Manet: Olympia (1863)

Fig. 18
Titian: The Venus of Urbino (1538)

Fig. 19
Daumier: In front of Mr. Manet's painting (1865)

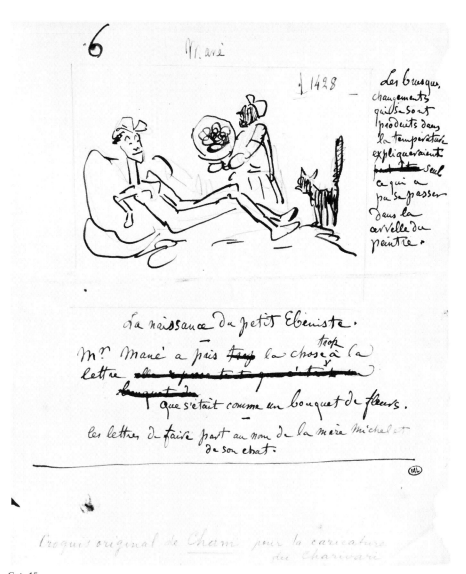

Cat. 15
Cham: Caricature of Manet's Olympia

divinities and nymphs hold measuring instruments resulted in a masterpiece of Kitsch. He lacked the weapon possessed by Manet, genius, nor was he able to bring a similar irony to his observations of the subject. Manet's *Old Musician* (1862) is at once a collage and a " profana conversazione " ; his *Olympia* (1865, *fig. 17)* is Titian's *Venus of Urbino, (fig. 18)* lying in a brothel.

In using this irony, he became one of the first artists to parody painting, that is to paint from painting itself. Manet, totally involved in his art, became himself the totality of what he represented, in somewhat the same way that Flaubert claimed to *be* Madame Bovary.

Zola translated ideally this magic convergence between the urgency of the raw form of painting and the composition " of the subject " : " ...The accuracy of the eye and simplicity result in a miracle; the painter proceeded as nature proceeds herself, through clear masses and large areas of light. His work has the harsh austere aspect of nature [...] a painting for you is a simple pretext for analysis. You needed a naked woman, so you chose Olympia, the first-comer; you needed bright luminous dabs of color, and so there you put down a bouquet of flowers; you needed black areas, and in a corner you placed a negress and a cat. What does it all mean? You have no idea and neither do I..." (1867).

The writer was one of the first to understand that Manet had rediscovered what the grandeur of the past masters really was: to produce a painting whose proper logic transcended the meaning of the aspects of life it represented. It was no longer the composition that dictated its significance to the objects and to the beings with which it was populated, but rather these very objects and beings that created composition by their existence on the canvas.

In this way an inexpressible grace invites the viewer to explore the degrees of emotion bordering the fine line between mystification and contemplation.

A recent Parisian exhibition *Raphael and French Art* (1983) has brilliantly demonstrated the inspiration that certain nineteenth century artists, among others, drew from the study of the Master of Urbino: from Ingres to Maurice Denis, from Horace Vernet to Degas and from Bonnard to Cezanne.

Within the limited framework of this section, short "flashes" can give some idea of the fragmented interpretation of Titian through three works that cover a period of fifteen years: **Fortune and the Young Child** (1857) by **Paul Baudry** *(cat. 1)* illustrates three celebrated lines from the fable by La Fontaine:

" ...And Fortune passed, awakening him gently
    And said: I have saved your life
    Be wiser the next time, I beg of you. "

Everything in this painting evokes (without entirely duplicating it) *Sacred Love and Profane Love* by Titian. Baudry thoroughly studied this painting at the Borghese Gallery in Rome. The sparse and suffocating elements, the fountain, the gracious *putto,* Fortune's unsteady attitude in slight *contrapposto,* her soft and pearly skin surrounded by the purple draperies, and above all the expression upon her face, are borrowed from the allegorical maiden holding a chalice on the right of Titian's painting. In Baudry's painting her position is reversed and Fortune's face is illuminated with a smile worthy of Leonardo da Vinci.

Baudry equally rediscovered the hazy texture of atmosphere peculiar to the Venitian Master that lightly veils the voluminous surfaces and renders this *sfumato* more delicate by creating a unity between the planes. An almost archaeological reconstruction, thoroughly appreciated by his contemporaries, this painting is an honorable example of a mid-century approach to the past masters, which a young artist awarded the Prix de Rome might attempt. He claimed that Titian, Tintoretto and above all Veronese were his preferred models for his cycle of paintings in the Great Hall of the Paris Opera House.

Cat. 1
Baudry: Fortune and
the Young Child

Cat. 4
Courbet: Nude with Dog

The tone is completely different for **Courbet's Nude with Dog** (1861, *cat. 4*). The provocation here is flagrant. Already in the celebrated *Bathers* of 1853, a painting which the Emperor was supposed to have whipped in a fit of rage at the Salon, Courbet transposed a recollection of Correggio's *Noli me Tangere* by inversing the order of the elements in the composition. By considerably reducing the volume of his palette, he superimposes numerous scattered references to Titian: *The Venus of Urbino* and especially *Danae (fig. 20)* of the Prado Museum. Instead of the golden rains, this modern Venus, showing no modesty, submits herself to the playfulness of her little Havanan poodle. The extraordinary transparency of the Venitian atmosphere which exalts the perfect oval of her naked body can not diminish the assertive vulgarity of the subject. This painting with its outright promiscuity preceeds a series of *galant* nudes that border on pornography, where Courbet proves his startling technical skill as well as his biting humor.

    Cézanne's Idyll (1870, *cat. 2*) presents a moment of instability in the evolution of his creativity that is absolutely fascinating. The allusion to the *Concert Champêtre (fig. 16)* at the Louvre, still attributed to Giorgione at the time, is

Fig. 20
Titian: Danae (1553-4)

Cat. 2
Cézanne : Idyll or Pastorale Scene

enriched by the refracted prism of Manet's corresponding *Déjeuner sur l'Herbe* which itself already ranked as a model of its kind. In the former, visual nostalgia is elaborated by a subtle irony. The man lying down facing the spectator is Cézanne himself, surrounded by his inseparable friends, Emile Zola and Baille besides the objects of their desire, ready to leave for some nearby Cythera, " a sad and black island " as Baudelaire imagined it.

Roger Fry proved to be affected by the gloomy severity of the scene, "...what funereal festivities do these Tintorettesque nudes celebrate in these sombre glades, in company with what preposterous ladies clothed in distorted caricatures of contemporary fashionable dress, with what obese and bald-headed bourgeois gentlemen ! "

Actually at this time Cézanne was standing at the crossroads of his creativity. His expressionist romanticism that exploded in *The Orgy* (1864) had calmed down, but he had yet to attain the Olympian serenity of his later years. Thus, the cloudy orbs cast into endless spirals become restrained and develop into irregular concentric circles which emanate from the island and its reflection in the water, to progressively embrace all the actors on the stage.

By use of a mobile spheric field of vision, Cézanne corroded the geometric perspective inherited from the Italian Renaissance ; here we have the first stage of his reconstruction of reality.

The grand classical themes to which he was still attached, such as in his *Déjeuner sur l'Herbe, Judgment of Paris* and *Temptation of Saint Anthony,* progressively underwent a virtual chemical transmutation. Losing their allegorical sense they became subliminated into metaphors. In this way, Cézanne could harmonize the exterior world with his interior vision.

Nudes

The drawing of nudes was the essential test of academic studies and was held as the priviledged expression of a superior ideal, the indisputable point of departure towards the great Greco-Roman historical compositions. The tangible reality of the model entirely disappeared behind the noble posture, copied from antiquity which was the form. The student was incited to employ all the subtilities of *chiaroscuro* upon an object that he already had a tendancy to idealize.

The small illustration for **Greek Interior** by **Gérôme** *(cat. 7)* (or *Scene of the Gynaeceum)* (1848) is an interesting example of the first stage of a composition ; it is freer and less worked than the final version. The four naked bodies have yet to lose their bulkiness, due to his concentrated work upon the detail, but one is pleasantly surprised by a certain sensuality derived from Ingres and a sense of the approach of Chasseriau's *Tepidarium* (1855).

Gérôme often revived this central figure particularly in the celebrated *Phryne before her Judges* (1861). His creations are mainly objects for public consumption upon which Zola secreted his venom : " Here the subject counts for everything, and the painting is nothing, a reproduction is worth more than this work [...]. There is no provincial drawing room where an engraving showing *A Duel After the Costume Ball* or *Louis XIV and Molière* is not hung ; in bachelor bedrooms we find *Almàh* and *Phryne before her Judges,* spicy subjects that can be permitted amongst men. More serious people have *The Gladiators* or *The Death of Cesar.* Monsieur Gérôme works for all predilections. He has in him a note of lasciviousness which livens up his dull and gloomy paintings. Furthermore, to hide the complete emptiness of his imagination he throws himself into worthless antiquity. He draws classical interiors like nobody else. This fellow poses as a knowledgeable and serious man. " (1867).

Contemporary research insists upon the role probably played in this type of painting by photographs of the nude and even the erotic stereoscopic photographs of models posing in various positions that were discreetly exchanged. Moreover, Ingres, Delacroix and Courbet did not hesitate to use photographed nudes that were naturally more static than real models ; but these documents have great trouble being accepted as artistic statements in their own right. Even when idealized, the photographic nude appears too trivial and shocking.

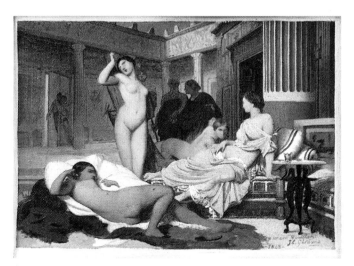

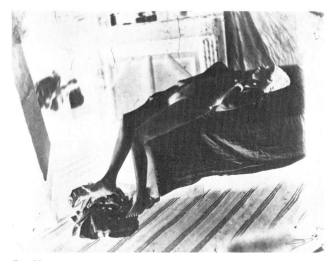

Cat. 7
Gérôme: Greek Interior

Cat. 26
Nègre: Nude in the Studio

Photography thus rivalled academism in the reproduction of young nudes. The **Nude in a Studio** (circa 1850) by **Charles Nègre** *(cat. 26)* totally escapes this servile tendency. The feeling of this young woman's extraordinary naturalness is seized as though she were completely unaware of the camera's presence as she lies on the edge of her bed, with her clothes rolled up at her feet. The oblique and plunging perspective accentuates the originality of this unprecedented composition, which predates the works of Degas and Toulouse-Lautrec by about thirty years.

With no special knowledge of this photograph, **Toulouse-Lautrec** expressed similar liberty of composition in **Alone** *(cat. 13)* (1896). In a few brushstrokes, he captured another model, most likely a prostitute, surrendering to her fatigue, dressed in her rumpled blouse and abandoned like a glove upon an unmade bed. He naturally identified with the outcasts of society, himself a welcomed regular visitor at the local brothels. He did not share the distant approach of the Naturalists by moralizing, and introduces us to this woman with whom he shared a profound affinity, in which compassion was balanced by humor. An extraordinary sketch, which Gustave Moreau declared " was painted entirely in absinthe ", *Alone,* announces the proffering of fallen women by Gustav Klimt and Egon Schiele.

The **Bathers** *(cat. 3),* like the *Mountain of Sainte Victoire* is a theme to which **Cézanne** relentlessly returns, a string of variations leading him to redefine the integration of volumes in space ; this at the twilight of his creative evolution.

This small painting (1892-1894) sets a group of bathers at the edge of the water, halfway between a fragmentary memory of reality and an evocation of mythology.

Cat. 13
Toulouse-Lautrec: Alone

Cat. 3
Cézanne: The Bathers

48

Cézanne did not impose an a priori scheme on the facts; he gradually developed his interpretation of this gathering of nudes through prolonged contemplation, of an either free or controled nature, that leads us to the essential heart of memory.

In his quest for a " harmony parallel with nature ", the painter in his later years seems to have found the emotive dimension of form, a sort of synthesis between volume and space which gives things, as Lionello Venturi noted, a sense of real duration, of prolonged existence within the consciousness.

Fig. 21
Dagnan-Bouveret: A Wedding at the Photographer's (Salon of 1879)

Photographic Portraits

The first " photographs " by Niepce, Daguerre and Talbot, before the invention of the word designated to identify this new process, were still lifes. This was due to the extremely long time required for posing; the first portraits meant a sitting time of fifteen to twenty minutes, and for the model it was true torture.

Despite this inconvenience, photography rapidly became a fashionable phenomenon, a sort of ritual that was almost an obligation. Daumier in numerous lithographs stigmatized the stilted bourgeoisie who rushed out to the photographers to have their pictures taken as " civilized men ". To confront this growing demand, the celebrated photographers opened their first studios to avoid the need to transport their fragile material and to facilitate experimentation with artificial lighting and the staging of an image. From 1854, fashionable Paris made its way to Nadar's workshop in order to belong to his celebrated *Pantheon*. Disdéri invented the " calling card " with the aid of his camera using numerous lenses to allow the client the choice of his favorite pose chosen from between six and nine photographic plates. He employed about one hundred people in his studio on the rue Lafitte, where the Emperor thought nothing of dropping in while his troops waited outside at the outset of their descent into Italy.

Most of the photographers were former painters, and not necessarily unsuccessful ones as Baudelaire contemptuously observed. The pioneers of photography applied the same rules of lighting inherited from Renaissance artists and clung to the stipulated conventions of portrait art concerning expression and posture.

A good example of academic posture without pomp or pretention is the **Portrait of the Painter Corot** by **Pierre Petit** *(cat. 27a)* (1860). The carefully studied and prepared pose appears to be a synthesis of different moments: the face, separated from the darkened bust by the white collar which illuminates it, is turned towards the spectator and looks into the distance, communicating some of the serene lassitude of an inspired genius. A true stakhanovite of ecclesiastic portraits (25,000 photo plates produced in 1864), the hard-working Petit only rarely attained the majestic balance of this photograph.

His **Portrait of Gustave Doré** *(cat. 27b)* can be contrasted with an older photograph by **Nadar** *(cat. 24)* (1855, developed by Alphonse Poitevin). The

Cat. 27b
Petit: Portrait of Gustave Doré

Cat. 29
Nadar: Portrait of Gustave Doré

Cat. 28
Robert: The Painter Troyon in his workshop

Cat. 30
Nadar: Portrait of a West-Indian

Cat. 20a
Feuardent: Portrait of Millet

Cat. 20b
Feuardent: Millet and his Family

effects of shade that clearly divide the dark from the light tones, the total absence of spatial references and the tortured look of *Jeune France* (the disheveled-looking Romantic generation) act out their roles in the composition with a thrilling and expressive romanticism.

Also by Nadar is the celebrated **Portrait of a West Indian** (1854-1859, *(cat. 25)* who was perhaps his servant, Rose. The young lady has adopted an allegorical pose which is entirely classical, as if she were the Muse of Photography. Nadar was able to fix on the plate the moment at which her charming face radiates all her interior being with a supreme calm. "The face is the soul of the body". Rarely had a portrait so completely endorsed Wittgenstein's aphorism.

Here photography seems to have been ahead of painting. It was necessary to wait for the Impressionist's portraits for the poses to appear completely informal. Renoir, in Bazille's portrait (1867) was captured at the moment when the painter had taken up a position of complete relaxation, his legs upon his chair as though he were alone unobserved. In the *Portrait of Mallarmé* (1876) by Manet, the poet is smoking a cigar and comfortably settled on the sofa. The absence of pathos demystifies the convention of the stiff portrait.

In the photograph by **Louis Robert** of **The Painter Troyon in his Studio** (1852 *cat. 28*), the painter who was known for his horror of having to pose is incredibly spontaneous — not only is there a complete absence of contrived facial expression on the subject's part, but the lighting equally gives no indication as to the artist's social function. The position of his hands has a particularly immediate and brutal accuracy, like the expression of a hunted "savage" that the photographer has been able to take by surprise.

Félix Feuardent in a daguerrotype of 1854 showing his friend **Jean-François Millet** *(cat. 20a and 20b),* accentuates the somber and introverted expression of the painter, which is no longer present in a group portrait taken on the same day, when he was surrounded by his devoted family.

Orientalism

By publishing his collection of poems *Les Orientales* (1829), Victor Hugo wiped out the two-dimensional Orient of the eighteenth century at one stroke — the Orient of Reason which exists in Montesquieu's *Persian Letters* (1719) as well as that of the fantastical imagery in Pétis de la Croix's *A Thousand and One Day* (1745), not to mention the paradisiacal and froliscome Orient of Mozart's *Abduction from the Seraglio.* Ever since the Romantic generation, the Orient, principally North Africa and Egypt, had grown more accessible after the dwindling of Ottoman power. These regions became the inverted double of the European imagination, the enchanted lands of desires that built up "beyond the mirror".

During his trip to Morocco and Algeria, Delacroix confirmed the inclination for flamboyant exoticism that he had already shown in *The Death of Sardanapalus* in 1827. He discovered there an unspoiled reflection of antiquity that Greece or Rome could no longer evoke. His repertoire was enriched considerably, but his conquests should be measured more in terms of his use of color. In his *Women of Algiers* (1830, *fig. 22*) the dazzling sunlight confirmed his use of pure color in shade.

Fig. 22
Delacroix: Women of Algiers (1832)

Fig. 23
Gérôme: The Prisoner (1861)

The following generation appears to have found what it was looking for. W. Holman Hunt undertook his quest for biblical man ; Charles Gleyre and in particular Léon Gérôme established a phantasmagorical Islam composed of religious modesty, refined sensuality, barbaric cruelty and passive submission. This Orient of unrelenting fatalism, where repressed European sexuality could abandon itself, was endowed with a huge literary success throughout the entire period, beginning with Hérédia's *Trophies* (his poem *Prisonner (fig. 23)* is dedicated to a painting of 1863 by Gérôme, that carries the same title) and later including *Les Pléiades* by Gobineau (1874) and Pierre Loti's *Aziyadé* (1879).

The Realist movement in the middle of the century seemed to incite the painters of the Orient to the rendering of a more ethnographic vision. Gérôme's students took pride in distinguishing with morbid accuracy architectural details as well as the different physical types. Despite his very close knowledge of North Africa, a painter such as **Fromentin** retained a style of romantic narration, similar to his travel accounts, *A Summer in the Sahara* (1856) and *A Year in Sahel* (1858).

From 1850 on, his reputation as an orientalist spread. He was one of the first

to appreciate the novel possibilities that the blinding desert light offered to painting. Scenes like that in the *Land of Thirst* (1869), where the sun drains the colors and bleaches everything white fascinated the Salon public. Even more celebrated, judging by the abundance of engraved reproductions, was his **Falcon Chase in Algeria — The Gathering of the Quarry** (1863, *cat. 5*) which permitted him to place the protagonist of his accounts, the Arab horseman, in an atmosphere that is for once peaceful. As Théophile Gautier noted, he did not portray the Arab experience as subservient, rather recreated it through the evocation of a medieval chivalrous ideal which was already on the wane. Fromentin concludes the period of Romantic Orientalism.

With the opening of the Suez Canal (1869) and the appearance of the first organized tours by Thomas Cook, it became necessary to travel to the Far East or to the South Sea Islands in search of virgin territory; however, Orientalism was not a short-lived phenomenon despite the pessimistic predictions of Castagnary. The Orientalists, trustees of a style of tourist painting where it was possible to inhale a scented souvenir of the bazaar, opened their Salon in 1894.

Auguste Renoir, on the trail of Delacroix, was amazed to discover the luxuriance of the Algerian vegetation and the beauty of its landscapes where "everything is white". He captured an **Arab Festival** *(cat. 10)* in 1881 with a panoramic use of space that is rare in his work, where hints of white are punctuated by ochre, red and violet brush strokes that vibrate, unifying the decor and the participants in the same scorching atmosphere. The impact of this chromatic exaltation was already visible in *"Le Déjeuner des Canotiers"*, painted just before his departure to North Africa.

Sculpture

Sculpture, far more narrowly dependant upon academic study of the human body and the achievement of the highest Canovian ideals of perfection, appeared resistant to the innovations of the mid-nighteenth century. The integration of the sculpted object in its surrounding space as well as its three dimensionality induced an independant study which emanated from the spatial redefinition achieved by painting on flat surfaces. Sculpture was moreover mainly created for exhibition in a public place, out of doors, and largely constituted the artistic education of the general public. It now seems as if it evolved more slowly than painting, with the exception of strong personalities such as Antoine Préault, whose bas-reliefs presented compositions in which a striking expressionism abolished any spatial conformity, or Carpeaux, who excelled both in the rhythmic dynamism of his sculptured groups and in the psychological penetration which he gave to the busts of his contemporaries.

The great adventure began with **Auguste Rodin** and the **Age of Bronze** (1877, *cat. 18*) which established his fame ; he himself believed throughout the long period during which the sculpture took shape, that it was his masterpiece (in the medieval sense of the word). After being shown in Brussels, the statue was presented at the 1877 Salon, where it was highly criticized : the art critic Charles Timbal saw in it " ...a curious studio study with a terribly pretentious title " (at that time *The Vanquished*). The ambiguity that arose around the title demonstrates Rodin's endless hesitations over his subject which he claimed embraced four different characters. Deprived of the patent attributes and clues as to meaning to which they had been accustomed, public and critics alike felt baffled. It seemed to them that perhaps this young athlete, half of whose face was hidden, pressed against his right arm, might be awaking from some kind of nightmare. There was no obvious explanation for the anguish of his features.

Rodin had intended to evoke the primitive being in the Jean-Jacques Rousseau sense, a physically perfect creature woken by the divine spark of life. The modeled perfection, the incredible realism of the tremour running through the body was so convincing that the sculptor was accused of encasing his model's body in a mold, a charge that he had no difficulty in repudiating. On the threshold of his long career, Rodin had struck the complacent world with a work of genius.

Cat. 18
Rodin: The Age of Bronze

Cat. 17
Maillol: Standing Bather

Objets d'art

Fig. 24
Donatello: David (c. 1440)

During the mid-nineteenth century a certain decadence of taste prevailed in the field of the decorative arts, as contemporaries frequently testified. Perhaps it was the "reign" of Percier and Fontaine, favorite decorators of Napoleon I and promoters of the "Empire Style" that led to this deterioration. The profusion of ornamentation and the repetition of motifs in their work resulted in a symbolic devaluation, and decorative concerns overtook those of space. Previously the cluttering of a room would have been inconceivable due to the high cost of objets d'art. Mechanization rapidly permitted the imitation of luxury objects, until then only hand-made : the mule-jenny considerably speeded up the weaving of carpets covered with floral patterns; the electrodeposition invented by the Russian Jacobi in 1837 permitted plaster and lead objects to be covered by a thin layer of metal. Flagrant bad taste incited the bourgeois to accumulate paintings and chromolithographs, marble and embossed metal statues, and furniture of every conceivable style *(fig. 25)*. A mid nineteenth century interior is generally recognizable by the confused mass of accumulated trinkets that soak up the oxygen. It is hard to imagine the celebrity that surrounded a silver smith like **F.D. Froment-Meurice.** The novelist Eugène Sue compared him to Cellini, apostrophizing him as "My dear Benvenuto," and Victor Hugo in one of his *Odelettes* wrote a hommage to him,

" (...) Poets or chislers
    Through us the spirit awakens.
    We render the good better
    You make beauty more beautiful. "

Fig. 25
Art-journal Illustrated Catalogue,
Crystal Palace, 1851

In treating a subject of this kind, he could have turned to the spectacular ethnography of Emmanuel Frémiet (1824-1910) whose *Stone-Age Man* was then fashionable ; instead he chose to follow in the tradition of Donatello *(fig. 24)* and Michelangelo, and retain the inner life of his idea.

Aristide Maillol, sculpted in his **Bather** (1900, *cat. 17)* a sort of modern-day *Koré*. Although his work is simply an unending series of variations on the female body, he naturally avoided the excesses of a gratuitous sensuality ready for consumption, which was the mark of recognition of Salon sculpture. Perhaps his petrifying love echos Théophile Gautier's phrase : " I have always preferred the statue to woman, and marble to flesh ". By divesting the model of her individuality, and by forbidding any movement which " unsettles the lines ", he eliminated the surface irregularities and permitted the light to run over the outside of the uniform mass. This solid and eternal beauty has been touched as much by a synthesis of Mediterranean archaism as by the sort of South-Sea primitivism that Gauguin might have endowed to Maillol : the *Koré* takes on some of the volume of a Polynesian wood carved idol.

Cat. 30a
Froment-Meurice: Silver Salver

Cat. 30b
Froment-Meurice: Silver Ewer

Cat. 16
Carrier-Belleuse: Hebe and Jove's Eagle

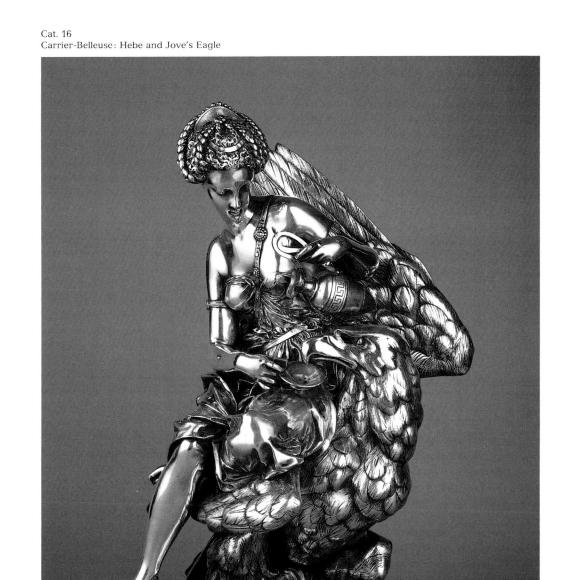

His celebrated **Toilette pour le Mariage de la Duchesse de Parme** (1845, *cat. 30 a and 30 b*) (Dressing table accessories for the Duchess of Parma) is like a paragon of the eclecticism that dominated of the period, when styles clashed in their overprofusion. The ewer and salver shown here were placed upon a silver tray in front of a neo-gothic mirror surrounded by candelabras, jewelery cases, etc. The ewer is covered with foliation, and on its ornamented side, two little Cupids bear the coat of arms of the newly-wed couple. The handle, on which another Cupid plays with a lizard, is in the form of a rose's stem. The ensemble could rival the Rococo chimera of François-Thomas Germain (1726-1791). Representing the French Decorative Arts at the 1851 World's Fair the *Toilette* by Froment Meurice captured the awe of the public, but not the admiration of the *Illustrated Catalogue's* critic " ...it's another example of the gratuitious extravagance which characterizes the French in this exhibition. The style is confused (...)."

Halfway between the objet d'art and sculpture (hybrid genres are another characteristic of this period) — **Hebe and Jove's Eagle** (1858) by **A.E. Carrier-Belleuse** *(cat. 16)* is a good example of the Second Empire Style, similar to the decoration of the Hotel Paiva on which the sculptor collaborated.

This mythological subject had already been treated by François Rude (1784-1855). There were those who believed that they detected in Hebe an allegory of a confidant France protected by the Imperial eagle. It is possible to see a sculpted translation of Correggio's or Parmigianino's sensual mannerism. The curvilinear softness of the design marries the vunerability of Hebe while the treatment of the silverplating emphasizes the feathers of the eagle.

In England a reaction to the dangers of mechanization at any cost was already being felt. Henry Cole, promoter of the Crystal Palace Exposition of 1851 was at the origins of concern for the necessary alliance between functionalism and beauty. With Ruskin he proclaimed a return to medieval craftsmanship and prepared the ground for the *Arts and Crafts* of William Morris.

The new style which was to impose itself upon the world from 1890 renounces corporatism, acquired specialization and value hierarchy between the artistic professions. Beauty was found in all, and the objet d'art determined to surprise the balance of nature's organic growth. The curved lines, the refusal of symmetry and the association of dissimilar materials, give expression to the secret fancies and the inexplicable tropism which troubled the nature awakened by Pan.

A perfect example of a language that was still finding its way is the **Vase by Rousseau and Léveillé** *(cat. 31)*. The wind which is spiraling over the surface agitates the floral decoration that adorns the neck of the vase, and the face of the Medusa surrounded by serpents forms a bronze mounting. The general feeling of movement gives great unity to this work of differing materials.

The porcelain **Vase by Otto Eckmann** (1897/1900, *cat. 29*) mounted in bronze reveals the pronounced symbolic stylization of mature Jugendstil. From the bulge of the vase to its neck the play of speckled colors evoke a chemical suspension controlled by the biological expansion of the leaves of the mounting.

Cat. 29
Eckmann: Vase

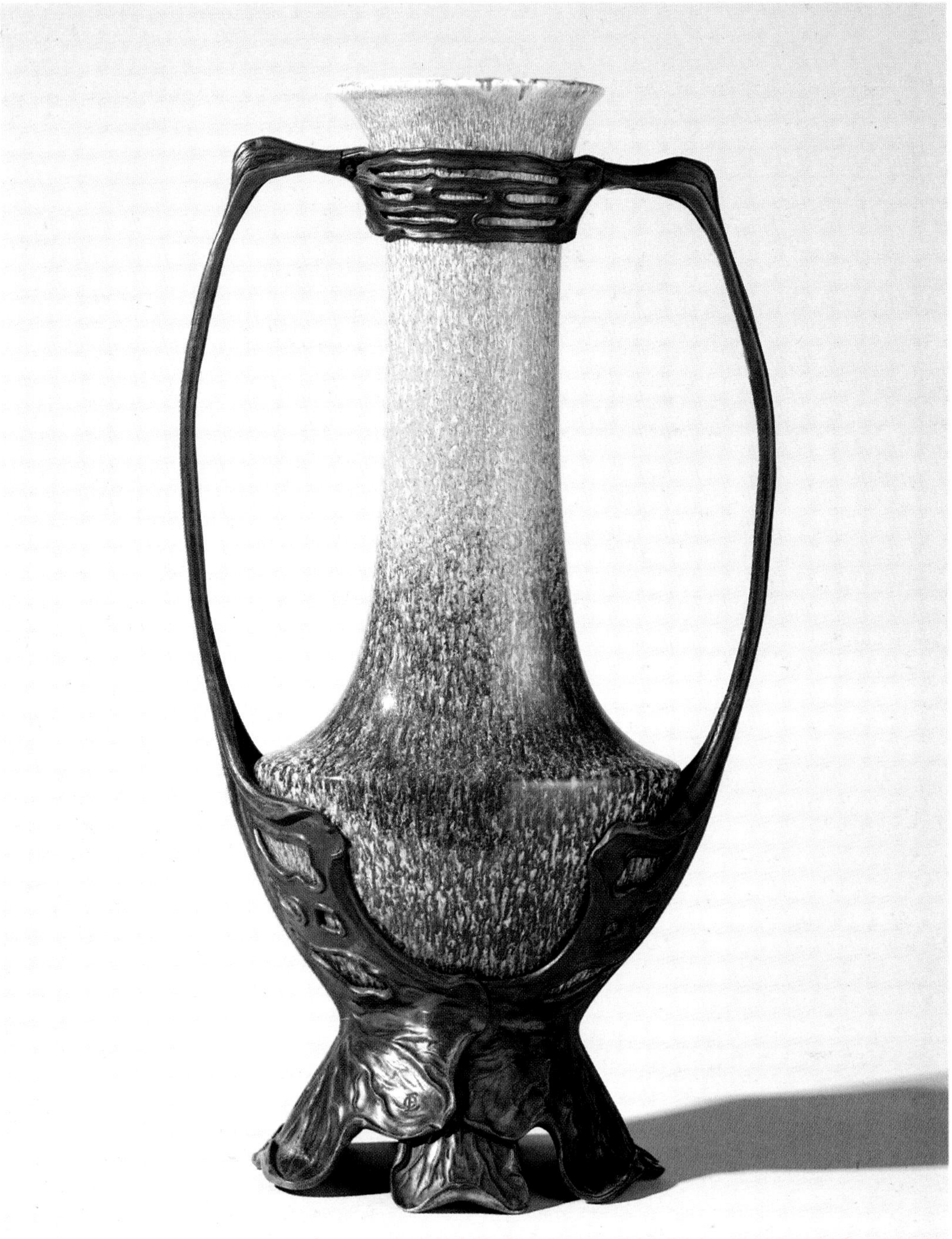

Paintings

Baudry Paul (1828-1886), French

1 *Fortune and the Young Child,* 1857
(La fortune et le jeune enfant)
Oil on canvas (194 × 146 cm)
Signed bottom right : *Paul Baudry*
Acquired at the 1857 Salon
RF 59

Cézanne Paul (1839-1906), French

2 *Idyll, or Pastoral Scene*
(Pastorale)
Oil on canvas (65 × 81 cm)
Former Pellerin Collection, Paris
Acquired by State in lieu of State taxes in 1982
RF 1982-48

3 *The Bathers,* 1894
(Baigneurs)
Oil on canvas (22 × 33 cm)
Former Pellerin Collection, Paris
Acquired by State in lieu of State taxes in 1982
RF 1982-41

Courbet Gustave (1819-1877), French

4 *Nude with Dog,* 1861
(Nu au chien)
Oil on canvas (65 × 81 cm)
Signed bottom left : *...68 G. Courbet*
Acquired by State in lieu of State taxes in 1979
RF 1979-56

Fromentin Eugène (1820-1876), French

5 *The Falcon Chase in Algeria - The Gathering of the Quarry*
(La chasse au Faucon - La curée)
Oil on canvas (162.5 × 117.8 cm)
Signed bottom right : *Eug. Fromentin*
Acquired at the 1863 Salon
RF 87

Gauguin Paul (1848-1903), French

6 *The Roman Burial Grounds at Arles*
(Les Alyscamps, Arles)
Oil on canvas (91.5 × 72.5 cm)
Signed and dated bottom left : *P. Gauguin, 88*
Gift of the Countess Vitali, 1923
RF 1938-47

Gérôme Jean-Léon (1824-1904), French

7 *Greek Interior,* 1848
Oil on canvas (15.5 × 21 cm)
Signed, dedicated and dated bottom right :
To my friend Douillard/J/L Gérôme 1848
Acquired in 1981
RF 1981-46

Mesdag Hendrik (1831-1915), Dutch

8 *Setting Sun* (1887 Salon)
(Soleil couchant)
Oil on canvas (140 × 180 cm)
RF 497

Monet Claude (1840-1926), French

9 *The Magpie* (La Pie) 1868
Oil on canvas (89 × 130 cm)
Signed bottom right : *Claude Monet*
Acquired in 1984
RF 1984-164

Renoir Auguste (1841-1919), French

10 *Arab Festival, Algiers. The Casbah,* 1881
(Fête Arabe à Alger-La Casbah)
Oil on canvas (73.5 × 92 cm)
Signed and dated bottom right : *Renoir 81*
Gift of the Biddle Foundation in memory of
Mrs Margaret Biddle in 1957
RF 1957-8

Rousseau Théodore (1812-1867), French

11 *Pathway in the Forest of the Isle-Adam,* 1849
(Une Avenue, forêt de l'Isle-Adam)
Oil on canvas (101 × 82 cm)
Signed and dated bottom left : *Th. Rousseau, 1849*
Chauchard Bequest, 1906
RF 1882

Sisley Alfred (1839-1899), English-French

12 *Snow in Louveciennes,* 1878
(Neige à Louveciennes)
Oil on canvas (61 × 50.5 cm)
Signed and dated bottom right : *Sisley, 78*
Camondo Bequest, 1911
RF 2022

Toulouse-Lautrec Henri de (1864-1901), French

13 *Alone,* 1896
(Seule)
Oil on cardboard (31 × 40 cm)
Signed bottom right : *H.T. L*
Gift of the Florence J. Gould Foundation, 1984
RF 1984-30

Van Rysselberghe Théo (1862-1926), Belgian

14 *Sailboats in the Estuary,* 1893
(Voiliers et Estuaire)
Oil on canvas (50 × 61 cm)
Signed bottom right : *VR*
Acquired in 1982
RF 1982-16

Sketch

Cham Amédée, Count of Noé, called (1819-1879), French

15 *Caricature of Manet's Olympia,* 1865
Pen and brown ink over traces of lead pencil
(22.9 × 18.3 cm)
Acquired at Public Auction, Paris 1983
RF 39.023

Sculpture

Carrier-Belleuse Albert (1824-1887), French

16 *Hebe and Jove's Eagle,* 1858
(Hébé et l'aigle de Jupiter)
Silver-plated bronze (51 × 31 × 30 cm)
Signed and dated on base on right : *A. Carrier. 1858*
Acquired in 1982
RF 3639

Maillol Aristide (1861-1944), French

17 *Standing Bather,* 1900
(Baigneuse debout)
Bronze (78 × 25 × 15 cm)
Monogram on the pedestal, left: *M*
Entered the public collections in 1949
RF 3250 - RFR 3

Rodin Auguste (1840-1917), French

18 *The Age of Bronze,* 1877
(L'âge d'airain)
Bronze (178 × 59 × 61.5 cm)
Signed on the pedestal: *Rodin*
Acquired at the 1880 Salon
RF 676

Photographs

Emerson Peter-Henry (1856-1936), English

19a *Marsh Leaves : The Waking River*
(6.5 × 9.5 cm)

19b *Marsh Leaves : Corner of a Farmyard*
(9.7 × 12.7 cm)
photogravure
Acquired in 1979
PHO 1979-74 and 762

Feuardent Félix, French

20a *Portrait of Millet,* 1854
Daguerreotype (14 × 9.8 cm)
Acquired in 1979
PHO 1979-60

20b *Portrait of Millet and his Family* 1854
Daguerreotype
(11.8 × 8.7 cm)
Acquired in 1979
PHO 1984-100

Fockedey Hippolyte (?-?), English

21 *Pavilion in a Parc,* 1853
(Pavillon dans un parc)
Negative paper (15.5 × 17.8 cm)
Acquired in 1983
PHO 1984-194

Hossard Professeur (?-?), French

22 *Paris Quays in the Snow,* 1843
(Quais de Paris sous la Neige)
Daguerreotype (7.5 × 10 cm)
Gift of the Kodak-Pathé Foundation, 1983
PHO 1983-65 (4)

De Meyer Adolphe, Baron (1868-1946), German

23 *Portrait of Alfred Stieglitz,* 1914
Platinum print
(23.5 × 18.7 cm)
Acquired in New York, 1980
PHO 1980-275

Tournachon Gaspar Félix, dit **Nadar** (1820-1910), French

24 *Portrait of Gustave Doré,* 1855
Photo lithography by Poitevin
(19 × 15.8 cm)
Acquired in 1984
PHO 1984-94

25 *Portrait of a West Indian* (1854-1859)
(Portrait d'une antillaise)
Salt print from collodion glass negative
(25 × 19 cm)
Signed and situated bottom left : *Nadar, 113,
(rue) Saint-Lazare*
Acquired in 1981
PHO 1981-37

Nègre Charles (1820-1880), French

26 *Nude in the Studio,* circa 1850
(Nu dans l'atelier)
Negative paper
(11.3 × 18.7 cm)
Acquired from the artist's family in 1981
PHO 1981-4

Petit Pierre (1832-after 1900), French

27a *Portrait of Camille Corot,* 1860
(25.1 × 19 cm)
Albumen silver print from collodion glass negative
Inscription on bottom left : *Pierre Petit, Photo* / bottom
right : *31 Rue Cadet, Paris*
Acquired in 1981
PHO 1981-43

27b *Portrait of Gustave Doré,* 1860
Albumen silver print from collodion glass negative
(25.5 × 18.2 cm)
Inscription bottom left : *Pierre Petit, Photo* / bottom right :
31 rue Cadet, Paris
Acquired in 1981
PHO 1981-42

Robert Louis (1811-1882), French

28 *The Painter Troyon in his Workshop,* 1852
(Le peintre Troyon dans son atelier)
Salt print from collodion glass negative
(24.3 × 18.5 cm)
Acquired in 1984
PHO 1984-90

Objets d'art

Eckmann Otto (1865-1902), German

29 *Vase,* circa 1897-1900
Porcelaine, patinated bronze (51.7 × 29 × 16 cm)
Signed twice upon mounting : *O.E.* interlaced
Acquired in 1982
OAO 539

Froment-Meurice F.D. (1802-1855), French

30a *Silver Salver,* 1847
(Bassin)
Partially gilded silver (47.4 × 34.6 × 3.9 cm)
Engraved signature reversed : *Froment Meurice*
Acquired in 1981
OAO 533

30b *Silver Ewer,* 1847
(Aiguière)
Partially gilded silver (41.3 × 21 × 19 cm)
Signed in hollow under the base : *Froment Meurice 1847*
Acquired in 1981
OAO 532

Rousseau Eugène (1827-1891)
Leveillé Ernest (known in Paris from 1859 to 1926)
and the **Escalier de Cristal** Workshop

31 *Vase,* circa 1890
Opaque and engraved glass, gold and silver plated
bronze
Acquired in 1980
OAO 513

Art and News Events

Solemnity and Caricature

Fig. 26
David: The Death of Marat (1793)

Seen with historical hindsight it appears that David's *Death of Marat* (1793, fig. 26) and his *Coronation of Napoleon* (1807, fig. 27) provide the first news reports of current events. From its beginnings this genre established lasting characteristics: the central position of a celebrated hero, the choice of a moment that would synthesize the complexity of the entire action, and a precision of detail that hinted at the portrayed reality. For David it was a question of giving an idealized account of important contemporary events in a manner that would narrow the gap between the present day and classical antiquity. In this way the event was presented as a quasi-religious celebration of rediscovered virtues. Following this hagiographic approach, the Romantic generation established a rupture by choosing its subjects from the controversies of the day in order to provoke reactions ranging from ecstasy to anger and indignation, as was the case with Delacroix's *Massacres of Scio* (1824), or to incite the guilty conscience of the public, as in Géricault's *The Raft of the Medusa* (1819, *fig. 28*). In these two paintings, the urgency of the message abolished the respectful distance which commemorative painting generally demanded. This new language concerned of horror, hallucination and hope, plunged the spectator into the abyss of the canvas. Painting no longer tried to convince by astounding, but rather by agitating and arousing the conscience. In this way, it implicitly refused to be an instrument of support for the establishment.

With **Daumier,** a participant in the Revolution of 1830, the point of permanent insurrection is reached by the image. Refering to caricatures like *Gargantua* (1831), *The Court of King Pétaud* (1832), and compositions such as *Transnonain Street* (1834, *fig. 29*), a variation on *The Death of Marat* ruthlessly secularized, Baudelaire remarked, " It is not exactly caricature, it is more the relating of a trivial and terrible reality. " Provocation earned Daumier repeated sanctions from the political powers: this remarkable group of caricatures not only attacked the conventional behavior of the new bourgeoisie but also the arrogance of bureaucracy; it still represents one of the most convincing

Fig. 27
David: The coronation of Napoleon (1807)

Fig. 28
Géricault: The Raft of the Medusa (1819)

Fig. 29
Daumier: Transnonain Street (1834)

Cat. 41
Daumier: Ratapoil

typologies of the abject. Of course caricaturization was nothing new, but no other artist, with the exception of Hogarth, had so completely devoted himself to the art to the point of concealing, as his contemporaries saw it, his natural genius as a sculptor and painter. With **Ratapoil** *(cat. 41),* which astounded Michelet, he depicted Bonaparte's agent as a foul, almost pathetic provocateur, always ready to entrap the Republican. The fascinating quality of this emaciated silhouette, Giacomettian before its time, is due to a balance between the comic and the repulsive that only Daumier knew how to maintain. When compared to his *Busts of members of parliament,* it is evident that some response deep within us is touched, possibly the heart of doubt itself. Daumier somehow managed to continue to publish his lithographs in *Le Charivari* during the Second Empire. Although he was no longer the ardent militant of 1830, his adherence to the revolution remained sincere, though veiled by a note of pessimism that his subsequent choice of subjects clearly reveals, especially the selection of the eternally defeated Don Quixote. He was no longer far from the deep-rooted scepticism of Flaubert, the relentlessly weary spectator of the February 1848 Revolution depicted in *The Sentimental Education* (1869).

Photography and the Press

The 1848 Revolution had an immediate effect upon the freedom of the press, and a need to know about events as they occurred grew continually. A new press with an increased circulation, financed by advertising, had appeared to satisfy the public's curiosity and its continually broadening field of interests. People realized that the destiny of the nation was not only controlled from the Tuileries and the Bourbon Palace, but also sprang from events in the Ottoman Empire, Algeria, the Papal States, and shortly the Crimea. From the Crimea, replacing the sporadic dispatches that had existed up until then, came the first eye-witness news reports. Journalists, watching from the hillsides, were allowed to give first hand accounts, despite the general mistrust of the military authorities. The English government had commissionned the photographer **Roger Fenton,** who used easily portable cameras and faster film (3 to 20 secs.), to report the Crimean War (1855) in which France, England, and Piedmont supported the Turkish Sultan against the Czar. However, at the explicit request of the English government he brought back 360 photo-plates in which there was no scene of action that might shock the public. His **Incidents in Camp Life** *(cats. 43a and 43b)* are somewhat pastoral and fabricated chronicals of what was to be one of the first modern wars.

Langlois, exercised a form of personal censure and, partly due to technical difficulties that should not be underestimated, he avoided battle scenes. His celebrated *Panorama (cat. 44)* of 14 photo-plates, as well as an astonishing image of the reknown **Wooden tower of Malakoff** *(cat. 45)* are a convincing ellipsis of the horrors of war which leave us with an impression of lunar desolation. Still

Cat. 43 a
Fenton: Group of Croat Chiefs

Cat. 43 b
Fenton: Camp at the 4th Dragon Guards

Cat. 44
Langlois: Panorama of Sebastopol
from the Tower of Malakoff

Cat. 44
Langlois: Panorama

Cat. 44
Langlois: Panorama

Cat. 45
Langlois: Wooden Tower of Malakoff

more striking were the photographs of Matthew Brady who covered the American Civil War, the first modern conflict in which urban dwellings became the target of military manœuvres, anticipating the civilian massacres to which the twentieth century would adapt, with their rows of corpses, calcinated ruins, disemboweled buildings, etc. *(fig. 30)*. Brady offered an unprecedented brutality, nullifying the gallantry of war so nobly celebrated in painting up to then, and instead unveiled atrocity in its crudest form. For the public, the real spectacle of death was unbearable. Brady ended his life a ruined man.

Fig. 30
Brady: Ruins in Richmond, Virginia (1865)

Although not always reaching the limits of the new technique's expressive possibilities, photography grappled with current events : not that newspapers were covered in photographs, or that they had a broader circulation ; reproductives techniques could as yet hardly print engravings from a photograph, but this new technical possibility became the advocate of truth, the essential basis of its elaboration. It is hardly surprising that photography is always associated with modern discoveries, as Baldus' *Railway Album* (1855), a true documentary of the railway testifies.

Whether concerned with unpleasant war scenes, the imperial family observed at an intimate moment, or the first steps of a new invention, photography eliminates all rhetoric and removes the residual indefinition of a written text.

Painting Modern Life

The importance of photography as a means of verifying reality in impressionist researches has often been alluded to . Roughly speaking it is possible to make a separation between paintings intended to represent a particular given moment which avoid political commitment, and commemorative paintings that claim to be eternal.

Fig. 31
Gérôme: The reception of the Siamese Ambassadors in Fontainebleau (1864)

It is here that an unbridgeable division is revealed between modernity and news. Despite their radically different ideological intentions, two paintings, *The Reception of the Siamese Ambassadors at Fontainebleau* by Gerôme (1864, *fig. 31)*, and *The Civil Marriage of Mathurin Moreau* by Gervex (1881, *fig. 32)*, originate from an identical solemnizing intention, where the almost photograhic precision of the gestures emphasizes their eternal quality. Compared to these paintings, any Monet garden scene, despite the banality of its subject and its casualness of inspiration, suggested a new way of looking at the world by eliminating contours and freely associating objects through light. This aroused the indignation of many contemporaries, reactionaries, liberals, and revolutionaries alike. Simply stated, a basin of water-lilies informs us better about our history than a painting of current events.

Of course, this does not mean that the painters of the avant-garde distanced themselves from their period : nobody was better than the Impressionists in keeping up to date. They all unpretentiously recorded daily activities : picnics on

Fig. 32
Gervex: The Civil Marriage of Mathurin Moreau (1881)

Fig. 33
Manet: The Barricade (1871)

Fig. 34
Manet: Clemenceau (1880)

the lawn, a bather's rest at the seaside, working class danses ; for them, no facet of social life was unworthy of a painting. Themes drawn from contemporary history were rare, and Manet was an exception in this field.

Manet's sources of pictorial inspiration could be prominent political events, social conflicts, or a passion for the urban scene. Examples are *The Battle between the Kearsage and the Alabama* (1867) which took place off the coasts of France during the Civil War, *The Execution of the Emperor Maximilian* (1867), for which the painter borrowed from photographs and *The Barricade* (1871, *fig. 33)*, a lithograph inspired by the dramatic events that he witnessed during the Paris Commune.

These works illustrate the strong sense of historical composition during his first creative period, if we are to consider 1867-1870 as a convenient turning point in his life. Up to then he relied more closely on past models. If, from then on, he moved in the direction of Impressionism, as is apparent in paintings such as *Argenteuil,* and *In the Boat,* as well as certain street scenes, he did not, however lose his taste for political life, as is clear from the portraits of *Georges Clémenceau* (1880, *fig. 34), Antonin Proust* (1880), his close friend and the future Minister of Fine Arts, and *Henri de Rochefort* (1881), the brilliant polemist and Empire provocateur, recently returned from exile after the amnesty granted by Gambetta.

Indeed the romantic **Escape of Rochefort** *(cat. 36),* was to be for Manet, an enthusiastic republican, his final reference to current events. This event had occurred seven years before ; the courageous escape of Rochefort and his friends from the prison in Noumea, where the *Moral Order* Republic had confined them for their part in the Paris Commune, dated from 1874. The fugitives are here seen from the shores of New Caledonia ; in the Zurich Kunsthaus version, Rochefort is clearly recognizable. Differing from the actual circumstances, he is at the helm in the back of the boat, which emphasizes his prominence as the hero of the adventure. In the version recently acquired by the Musée d'Orsay, on exhibit here, the party has already left the docks, as if in the second take of an imaginary film, where none of the fugitives aboard are recognizable. There is only the fragile skiff, seen from above, floating upon an electric and phosphorescent sea, a sort of Ravelian *Barque on the Ocean,* radiating in the night, somewhere between the *Raft of the Medusa (fig. 28),* (to which the point in the background surely alludes), and Monet's *Impression, Soleil Levant* (1872). By refusing all dramatization of these romantic events, where the protagonists dissolve into their marine environment, Manet reveals his freedom to interpret a political event by showing his disenchantement with Rochefort's demagogic and anti-semitic nature, rather than portraying him as an upright Republican. The profound solitude of this melancolic *Escape,* perhaps also evokes lost illusions.

The Impressionists, completely occupied with the celebration of modernity in urban life, left politics alone ; even the ardent socialists such as Pissarro or bourgeois conservatives like Degas ; indeed all were avowed republicans, a position that became during the Third Republic a rather vague act of faith. In this

Cat. 36
Manet: Escape of Rochefort

Cat. 37
Monet: Rue Montorgueil with Flags

way, **Monet's Rue Montorgueil with Flags** (1878, *cat. 37*) painted to celebrate the festivities accompanying the 1878 World's Fair (on June 30th and not July 14th as previously believed), was one of the rare commemorative impressionist paintings, offered at the time when France was still suffering from its defeat against Prussia. In it he joined the far more labored patriotic spirit of Meissonnier's *Siege of Paris* (1873, *fig. 35*), or Puvis de Chavanne's *The Pigeon* (1871). Nevertheless, we cannot avoid the thought that Monet was particularly struck by the chromatic effervescence engendered by the myriad of flags fluttering at the caprice of the wind ; the vibrant color and rapid brush strokes, together with the plunging perspective of the cobblestone street, explode beneath the tricolored banners.

Fig. 35
Meissonnier : The Siege of Paris (1871)

Almost all of the great painters at the end of the century found inspiration in the bursts of pure color provided by the Republican celebrations, from Douanier Rousseau to Van Gogh, from Bonnard to the Fauvists : in this they announced the American Pop generation's use of the *Stars and Stripes,* a use whose corrosive irony does not always dissolve a certain underlying nostalgia.

At the close of the century personalities as diverse as Comte, Taine, Darwin, Ruskin and Nietzsche, contributed to the elaboration of a secular system of values, while the Third Republic established itself, defying the many threats it had received at its birth. Like every young regime, it called for artists to propose edifying imagery. Courbet and Champfleury were presented as the founding fathers of a new aesthetic order. Realistic subjects, previously judged as unworthy, swept into the Salon, although they were still treated in a traditional manner.

The Academy took refuge in the celebration of republican virtues : the progress of science and of enlightenment, economic prosperity and bourgeois prudence, sympathy for the poor and the work ethic. The Nation's glory was exalted, although in as secular a manner as possible, and of course, hope was expressed for a just revenge on the enemy. Republican realism found zealots in artists like Gervex, Bastien-Lepage (1848-1884), Detaille (1848-1912), Girardet (1853-1907), Falguière, and the writer Zola, who became its ardent prophet, believing in the reconciliation of impressionism, illusionism, and modern life.

Despite the amnesty proposed by **Gambetta,** the founder of a stable Republic, whom **Falguière** *(cat. 42)* sculpted in a handsome **Clay Bust (1884),** the Paris Commune remained a wound that the French political subconscious tried to forget. The price paid by Courbet for his part in the insurrection had indeed been costly. Those terrifying repressive times are recalled in **Clarin's Fire at the Tuileries** (1871, *cat. 33),* a vigorous sketch in which it is not yet possible to imagine the heavy decorative systems which the painter was later to present at the Hotel de Ville, the Sorbonne and the Opéra. Seen from the corner of the Conciergerie on a barricade covered by corpses, a female figure, reminiscent of Delacroix's " Liberty ", turns to contemplate the smoldering ashes that represent the vestiges of the Monarchy. The red flag is torn, but better times are announced.

It was on the same void left by the Tuileries that the architect **Lheureux**

Cat. 42
Falguière: Gambetta

Cat. 33
Clairin: Fire at the Tuileries

planned to raise a **Monument to the Glory of the French Revolution** *(cat. 40)*. It was to have been a symbolic expiatory temple in the form of an Aztecan or Ninivite pyramid, surrounded by porticos, columns, and fountains, signifying the final triumph of the Republic over obscurantism.

News and Social Events

For a long time France remained isolated and humiliated in Europe. The blue line of the Vosge Mountains, then in German hands, marked the limit of the political horizon. The consequence of the defeat was a closing in of France upon herself; the creation and building of an immense colonial empire was hardly enough to alleviate the humiliating pain, and the concept of colonialism had yet to find favor with the public. It was a dispute with England over Fashoda, an island on the Nile, that aroused the national sentiment. Attention concentrated on parliamentary life studded with its inevitable scandals (the trading of medals in which the President

Cat. 40
Lheureux: Monument to the Glory of the French Revolution

Cat. 34
Devambez: The Assault

Fig. 36
Vallotton : The Demonstration (1893)

was implicated, the collapse of the Panama Canal shares, bribary, and so on) ; while larger passions were unleashed by the *Affaires* : the struggle for power by General Boulanger (1889) and the polemics surrounding Captain Dreyfus (1894-1899).

A intriguing painting, **The Charge of Police** by **Devambez** 1902, *cat. 34*), dates from the aftermath of the Dreyfus Affair. A frequent visitor to the many artist studios found at the top of Paris apartement buildings, he took a liking to their aerial views, and painted garden scenes, playgrounds and street scenes, that recall the paintings of Vuillard. In *The Charge (fig. 36)*, he organizes a vertiginous aerial representation of the riot. The police cordon, closing in on the somber inarticulate mass of demonstrators who flee the brutality of the gendarmerie, the gloomy tonality of the scene ignited by only a few dabs of color, and the cold and ironic objectivity of this bird's eye view bring to mind the crowd scenes of Gustave Doré, and preceed the scenes of urban agitation treated by the Italian Futurists and the German Expressionists.

In the satirical newspapers, this tone of biting irony was transformed into violent derision : two newspapers, *Le Rire* and the *Assiette au Beurre (figs. 37, 38, 39),* irritated the satisfied bourgeoisie and their institutions with their sarcasm. Their favorite targets were clericalism, the army, and the jingoistic vengence of patriotism. Frequently caracturists, among whom painters like Toulouse-Lautrec, Vallotton, Steinlein and Ibels should be included, attacked the foreign monarchies. French diplomacy, which had for a long time existed in isolation, found itself in need of alliances and forced to court the sovereigns : **Iribe in his Military Parade in Vincennes** 1905, *cat. 38*) alludes to the Paris visit of King Alphonso XIII, and **Roubille's** vignette, " **Tell me little father, how do you want to be eaten ?** " *(cat. 39),* represents the Russian bear, who, wounded by the Japanese victory, turns to devour the Czar, shown as the ridiculous figure of a circus tamer (1905).

Fig. 37
How is France seen from abroad ? / — Next !
(1906)

Fig. 38
The Academy Inspector
(1906)

Fig. 39
— *Do* I *jump over the wall ?*
(1903)

Cat. 38
Iribe : Military Parade in Vincennes

Cat. 39
Roubille : The Wounded Russian Bear

The Franco-Russian alliance, a major axis of French foreign policy, found a more complacent illustrator in **Henri Gervex,** who left for Moscow in 1896 to paint **The Coronation of Emperor Nicolas II** *(cat. 35).* In his " Memoirs ", published in 1924, Gervex gave details capable of moving shop girls to tears. ("... What ardour in the Moujik's faces, what religousness in their entire attitude... ") It was as though he anticipated the TV reports that deal with social events, blending tasteful remarks with bell boy's confidences : The Czar (..." very simple... talking to my wive and I, asking a thousand questions about my work "...) was extremely pleased with the results. But the enormous work, ten meters long, was typical of the World's Fair's monsters, which tried to emulate Tintoretto, and found no panel in the St. Petersburg palaces large enough to receive it. The sketch exhibited here, gives a fairly good idea of a form of painting that remained celebratory, and as yet unsupplanted by photography, that was destined to be reproduced in the newspapers and reviews. For Gervex, as well as for his public, there was no doubt that in his *Coronation of Nicolas II,* he had revived the grandeur of David's *Sacre de Napoléon (fig. 27).* One could be overwhelmed by the progress of science and technology, but a mere imitation of David's pageantry sufficed to add another link to the worshipped chain of tradition. This blindness might appear absurd if the twentieth century dictatorships had not organized a vicious and cunning alliance between technical modernity and ultra-reactionnary aesthetiscism. Karl Marx had already anticipated this situation with his feeling for concise formulas : " All repetition transforms drama into comedy. "

Cat. 35
Gervex: The Coronation of Emperor Nicolas II

Gruesome Reality

News reports, using the newest means of communication (telegraph, long distance daguerrotype, and the wireless), considerably enlarged the confines of the public's political consciousness. Nevertheless, one domaine always revives interest and becomes an important element in any thorough discussion of news : the sensational treatment of scandalous news items, inherited by the big circulation popular press from an oral folk tradition. Like a worn-out fable, with its naive tints of traditional regional imagery, the crics of hcinous crimes were heard : severed bodies stuffed into trunks, vengeance with arsenic, red-light taverns, jealous husbands and children burned after receiving their first communion.

These petty articles inebriated the masses not only because they touched the deeply rooted myths within the collective conciousness, but also because they proposed a flamboyant and dreadful marginality that existed right next door.

The *brief news items* were the domain of newspaper illustrators, caricaturists, and of genre painters. The great artists rarely ventured into this realm.

Cézanne's Strangled Woman *(cat. 32)* is an exception ; a last concession to the agressivity of his *couillarde* period. The strong contrasts of light and shade, the vitality of his execution, and the torture to which he submits the bodies, are all expressionist elements which foreshadow Kokoshka and Nolde, betraying his inability to subliminate through art the macabre and sexual fantasies with which he was beseiged. As if he believed in a magic, somewhat sadistic fulfillment of his desire to destroy the object (which we are led to believe in as well), he creates a whirling chaos, smothered by the crimson curtains that cry out the urgency of his impulse. The reality of these news briefs, the hypothetical starting point of the vision, dissolves into the interiorization of the gesture, thereby freeing the expression from the event.

Painting

Cézanne Paul (1839-1906), French

32 *The Strangled Woman,* 1872
(La Femme Étranglée)
Oil on Canvas (31 × 24.8 cm)
Donated by Max and Rosy Kaganovitch in 1973
RF 1973-11

Clairin George (1843-1919), French

33 *Fire at the Tuileries,* 1871
(L'Incendie des Tuileries)
Oil on Canvas (48 × 79 cm)
Signed, dedicated and dated towards the right ; *to my friend Geneviève, G. Clairin, May 1871*
Acquired in 1981
RF 1981-31

Devambez André (1867-1943), French

34 *The Assault,* (1902)
(La Charge)
Oil on Canvas (127 × 161.7 cm)
Signed bottom left : *André Devambez*
Aquired in 1979
RF 1979-61

Gervex Henri (1852-1929), French

35 *The Coronation of Emperor Nicolas II,* 1896
(Le Couronnement de l'Empereur Nicolas II)
Oil on Canvas (116 × 151.5 cm)
Acquired at the Salon de la Société Nationale des Beaux Arts in 1909
RF 1977-184

Manet Édouard (1832-1883), French

36 *Escape of Rochefort,* 1881
(Évasion de Rochefort)
Oil on Canvas (80 × 76 cm)
Signed bottom right : *Manet*
Acquired in 1984
RF 1984-158

Monet Claude (1840-1926), French

37 *Rue Montorgeuil with Flags,* 1878
(La rue Montorgueil)
Oil on Canvas (81 × 50.5 cm)
Signed bottom right : *Claude Monet*
Aquired by State in lieu of State taxes 1982
RF 1982-31

Illustrations

Iribe Paul (1883-1935), French

38 *Military Parade in Vincennes,* 1905
(La Revue de Vincennes)
Proof sketch with aquarelle highlights (26 × 42 cm)
Signed bottom left : *" Paul Iribe "* : Left inscription : *" a bit lighter on the heads "*
Acquired at Public Auction, Paris, 1983
RF 39017

Roubille Auguste (1872-1955), French

39 *The Wounded Russian Bear,* 1905
(L'ours russe blessé)
Proof sketch with aquarelle highlights (19 × 26.2 cm)
Initialed bottom right : *A.R.*
Acquired at Public Auction, Paris, 1983
RF 39020

Architectural Drawings

Lheureux Louis-Ernest (1827-1880), French

40 *Monument to the Glory of the French Revolution*
Pencil, pen, wash, aquarelle and gold highlights (48 × 86.5 cm)
Acquired at Public Auction, Paris 1981
ARO 1981-877

Sculpture

Daumier Honoré (1808-1879), French

41 *Ratapoil,* 1850
    Bronze (43.5 × 15.7 × 18.5 cm)
    Acquired by the Luxembourg Museum in 1892
    RF 927

Falguière Jean-Alexandre (1831-1900), French

42 *Gambetta,* 1884
    Terra-cotta (50 × 27.5 × 24 cm)
    Signed, on the pedestal: *A. Falguière*
    Acquired in 1926
    RF 1892

Photographs

Fenton Roger (1819-1869), English

43 *Incidents in Camp Life,* 1856
    Salt print from collodion glass negative
    a) Group of Croat Chiefs
    b) Camp at the 4th Dragon Guards
    (59.3 × 42.1 cm)
    Acquired at Public Auction, London, 1982
    PHO 1982-5 & 62

Langlois Jean-Charles (1789-1870), French

44 *Panorama,* 1855 (five of fourteen views)
    Paper negative (35 × 31 cm)
    Purchased in 1982 through a grant from the *Mission pour le patrimoine photographique*
    PHO 1982-21/210

45 *Wooden Tower of Malakoff,* 1855
    Paper negative (33.8 × 31.9 cm)
    Inscription written by hand bottom center during mounting: *Wooden Tower,*
    Acquired in 1982
    PHO 1982-30

Legray Gustave (1820-1882), French

46 *1852 Salon,* 1852
    Salt print from negative paper
    (18.6 × 21.6 cm)
    Acquired in 1983
    PHO 1983-166

"Correspondences"

" O silent mirrors of truth.
At the Ivory temple of solitude
Appears the reflection of cursed angels. "

Georg Trakl
Nocturnal Chant

A manifesto does not give birth to a movement, and the case of Symbolism is no exception. Even if the famous text by Jean Moréas *(Symbolism, a Literary Manifesto,* which appeared in the *Figaro* on September 18th, 1886) included a number of key phrases : " All concrete phenomena can not be revealed by themselves ; they are mere susceptible appearances assigned to represent their esoteric affinities with primordial ideas. " Even if the splendor of the movement is linked to the last decade of the nineteenth century, the source of its idealistic beliefs must be looked for in the earlier works of Baudelaire and Gustave Moreau. The scattered influences of Symbolism are felt deep in the heart of our own century, in the origins of Abstract Art, Surrealism, and Expressionism.

Radiating around the years of full expansion, Symbolism expressed a reaction against the materialism hovering over European culture. The rejection was directed at a scientific and technical society as well as the liberal and positivist ideology. Since man had been reduced by progress to a mere biological mechanism, it was vital to invoke the forces which animated the consciousness. Thus, absolute priority was given to the unexpressed, to dreams, to mental associations and to intuition.

Confronted with the certitudes of rationalism, Symbolism awakened the buried aspirations of the esoteric, the unreal, and the slumber of death ; it was a matter of rediscovering and restoring life to a feeling of nostalgia for the origins of mankind's shattered unity. Consequently, painting, music and poetry joined together and tried to celebrate the universe through the purest as well as most monstrous of its extremes. Around them gravitated *a limited number of fundamental themes* : the mystical union of man and woman, the osmosis between human beings and nature, and the achievement of love through death *(fig. 40).* From here, there derived *an unprecedented abundance of images,* which formed the frame of these intersecting preoccupations, and came to constitute the customary landscape of Symbolism : streams of gems, aquatic meanderings, artificial vegetation, knights, maidens, and so on... A vocabulary withered through centuries of use. Symbolism, in fact, revived this wearied syntax to offer an iconic substance to the impulsions of the dream.

Preceeding the *Manifesto* of 1886, the breakthrough undoubtedly dates from the publication of **Joris-Karl Huysmans's « A Rebours »** *(cat. 61).* (*Against Nature,* 1884), a manual for the extremely decadent ; the same *Yellow Book* that would influence Dorian Gray so intensely. Huysmans modeled his hero, Duke Jean Floressas des Esseintes, who organized his life like a work of art, on the **Count Robert de Montesquiou** *(cat. 56).* Through Des Esseintes, he proposed a very complex system of tastes and aspirations which aimed at the destruction of the naturalism so dear to Zola and his Médan Circle. On a daily basis, des Esseintes accomplished the " derangement of all sense " proclaimed by Rimbaud. He bathed in intoxicating exhalations, gave himself up to morbid languor, and summoned the high priests of the Symbolist Church to his phantasmagorical museum ; from Moreau to Redon, from Poe to Villiers de l'Isle-Adam, all helped him to " open the paradise of pure sensation. " Impressionism was among the

Fig. 40
G. Moreau : Orpheus (1865)

Cat. 56
Troubetzkoy: Robert de Montesquiou

victims of this new behavior : " Nature has had her day ; she has finally and utterly exhausted the patience of sensitive observers by the revolting uniformity of her landscapes and skyscapes ".

The confusion between mysticism and sensuality was one of the main points of departure for the rejection of materialism. Ambiguity, first of all, permitted truth to harmonize opposed concepts, as far removed from directly perceived reality as possible. Here we find the path laid out by Baudelaire in his poem *Correspondences* :

> " Like long echos from afar blending
> In a shadowy and profound unity
> Vast as night and as clarity
> Scents, colors and sounds answer each other. "

This ideal crystallization of meaning incites the breaking up of separate artistic languages and their harmonization which allows us to see reflected essential mysteries.

Fig. 41
Gauguin: Mallarmé (1891)

The poet, like the painter, crossing the forest of signs, attempts to give direction to the haphazard by awakening dormant archetypes, not by demonstration, analysis or analogous juxtaposition, but by suggestion, as defined by Mallarmé *(fig. 41)* : " To name an object is to take away three-quarters of the pleasure from a poem that is meant for gradual discovery. A suggestion, that is to dream. It is the perfect usage of this mystery which constitutes the symbol : evoking an object little by little, revealing a mood or, on the contrary, choosing and sounding out a mood through a series of interpretations. "

From this comes the incredibly simple language of Maeterlinck (1862-1949), under which are concealed the most haunting and inexpressible memories ; also the " non-finito " by Rodin, with its carved figures that seem reluctant to leave the chaos of the stone. And also from this proceed the multi-colored fabrics and damasks in which Klimt (1862-1918) smothers his figures *(fig. 42)*.

Suggestion supposes that the object is not completely revealed ; and in this way, the Symbolist artist shows the precise moment at which the object seems to break away from the mass that constrains and determines it ; it is almost as if the same object creates an environment in order to conceal itself. The result is a *decorative domain of the dream* which speculates upon the spiral, the curve, the serpentine line, the fusion of animal and vegetable, etc. This decorative domain comes to the fore in Art Nouveau.

Fig. 42
Klimt: Water Serpents (1907)

Expressive forms preserve the ambiguity of the myth, with a tendency towards abstraction that opposes the encroaching tin-clad imagery. Adolphe Retté, an orthodox symbolist, denounced these in 1899 : " Vermillion helmeted heroes pursuing intangible visions, slender and shivering knights, troubadours under the balconies of satanical princesses, gelatinous mermaids, humming shepherds... " Terms with which Symbolism has for too long been improperly associated.

In its most profound expression, Symbolism raises a vast semantic field of doubt : experienced anxiety confronted with the disorder of its surrounding directs its disparate forces towards an annihilation of art, the price that must be paid to ensure the definitive triumph of the idea.

Wagner

Baudelaire and Liszt were among the first to be converted to Wagner's music. The former immediately appreciated the deep range of sound sensations. Speaking of **Tannhäuser** *(cat. 63),* performed at the Paris Opera in 1861, the poet stated : On hearing the first bars, I remember having undergone one of those pleasurable sensations that almost all imaginative men have experienced in their dreams. I felt freed from *the confines of gravity* and I rediscovered the extraordinary *sensuality* that hovers *in the summits* (...) I then involuntarily pictured the delicious condition of a man in quest of total and absolutely secluded reverie, but a seclusion possessing *immense horizons,* full of *strong diffused light ;* immensity with no other decor but itself. Soon I felt a sensation of vivid *clarity,* the *intensity of the light* growing with such rapidity, that the nuances furnished in a dictionary could not suffice to express *this continual renaissance of ardor and whiteness.* I then clearly

Fig. 43
Original score of *Tannhäuser,* the ballet, Paris Opera, 1861

Cat. 63
Chaperon : Model for Wagner's *Tannhaüser*

Cat 47
Fantin-Latour: Isolde in the Tower

Fig. 44
Beardsley: The Wagnerites (1894)

imagined the idea of a soul wandering amidst light, ecstatic from *sensuality and knowledge* soaring above and far beyond the natural world." He continues by stating that Wagner is the most extraordinary painter of depth and space.

An art that combines the maximum expressiveness of song, orchestral discourse, theatricality, miming and stage-sets, Wagnerian drama is a total work of art, an abyss of dream, a labyrinth of mythical images. "It sometimes seems, when listening to this ardent and despotic music, that we are close to the vertiginous experiences of opium, painted against the backdrop of darkness, torn by reverie."

Long before the *Symbolist Manifesto,* Wagnerian lyrical drama stood for the perfect fulfillment of idealistic aspirations; it dictated a sensibility.

The first generation of pilgrims, around Villiers de l'Isle-Adam, Judith Gautier and Catulle Mendès, zealously went to the opening of the *Festspielhaus* in Bayreuth (1876). Accompanying them was **Fantin-Latour** who attempted to convey by pictorial language the emotion which overwhelmed him during the

Cat. 48
Fantin-Latour: Siegfried and the Rhine Maidens

operatic ceremonies. Noteworthy amongst his many sketches is one of **Isolde in the Tower** *(cat. 47)* seen from behind, waving her veil in the direction of Tristan, while holding in her other hand the burning torch that rages through the night. Far from reproducing the commonplace, rather dreadful stage setting of Bayreuth, he attempted to express a mental theater animated by a music which is sufficiently demonstrative in itself, with a rather latin sensibility. This is even more apparent in **Siegfried and the Rhine Maidens** *(cat. 48)* taken from the *Twilight of the Gods,* a scene which strangely evokes the Judgement of Paris.

The works which most struck the French-wagnerian coterie were without a doubt *Tristan,* a nocturnal hymn to the accomplishment of love through death,

Fig. 45
The Rhinegold, First Act

Fig. 46
Fantin-Latour : The Rhine Maidens (1876)

and *Das Rheingold (fig. 45),* in which the dramatic art is entirely original : there are no heroes, no love story, etc. If we had to limit ourselves to one wagnerian burst that resounds throughout Symbolism, a good example would be the *Rhine Maidens (fig. 46),* just as they are introduced by their musical score, with their theme originating in the movements of the primordial waters. Fantin-Latour devotes numerous pastels and lithographs to them, in which the spiraling movements of the three intermingled bodies reveal aquatic impulses. This same theme of the female body is found in the wave, the sea foam of all Art Nouveau creation, and is one of the essential images of the pantheistic creed.

Numerous representations of the sacred triad exist from Puvis de Chavannes' *Maidens on the Sea-shore* (1879, fig. 47), to Maurice Denis' *Trinity Evening* (1891) (in which the mythical Parcae superimpose the Three Graces) ; they seem to possess, in their apparent candor, the key to human destiny. Musical quotations from the *Rhine Maidens* abound in music, from the chorus of Debussy's *Sirènes* (1899), to the final movement of Holst's *Planets* (1914), as well as the soothing interventions of Turandot's attendants in the first act of Puccini's opera (1924). The foliation is endless, as the intertextuality abolishes the barriers between the different genres.

It was not surprising therefore that Edouard Dujardin, director of the *Wagnerian Review* (1885-1888), established Wagner as the founder of Symbolism. Around his publication he gathered the idealist generation : Mallarmé, Verlaine, Laforgue, Moréas, Régnier, Dukas, Chausson, Fantin-Latour, and strangely enough, Renoir, who in 1882, was sent by the Parisian Wagnerians to Palermo to execute a portrait of the master *(fig. 48)* that the model qualified as the " embryo of an angel ", no doubt due to the predominance of pink and blue.

Despite his reluctance, Wagner became the epicenter of this specifically French Wagnerian movement. At the end of his life, the magician of Bayreuth, achieved in *Parsifal* the chef-d'œuvre that Symbolism never dared to expect. The

Fig. 47
Puvis de Chavannes : Maidens on the Sea-shore (1879)

Fig. 48
Renoir : Wagner (1882)

turbid pleasures of sonority cultivated for its own sake, the heightened chromatism, the interior quality of an action torn between religion and eroticism attained a sort of parousia of mystery. Through its musical qualities alone, *Parsifal* was able to win the complete admiration of even the most reticent, as Debussy said, " We find here unique and unexpected orchestral sonorities. It is one of the most beautiful monuments that has ever been erected to the serene glory of music. " (1903)

As a result the *total work of art* was partly the source of movements as diverse as synthetic symbolist theater, Gustave Mahler's monumental symphonies, reverberating all the echos of the universe, as well as the ceremonies of Scriabin. Debussy, perhaps the most symbolist of musicians, kept a certain radical distance from Wagner : " ...these characters with helmets and hides become unbearable after the fourth evening (...) ; to think that they never appear without their damned *leitmotif,* and some even sing it ! " (1903).

From now on the prophetic stature bestowed upon Wagner began to subside giving place to a more tempered admiration for the musician's genius, and for the inspiration of the man of theater.

Fig. 49
Wagner : Tristan, First act

Salome

At the start there was hardly anything ; a few verses in the Gospel about this young princess urged on by her mother, Herodiade, to claim the head of Saint John the Baptist. The amplification of the anecdote does not date from the nineteenth century. The Venetians, Titian in particular *(fig. 50),* had already enlarged the subject. The disciples of Caravaggio followed suit, especially the very perverse Francesco del Cairo *(fig. 51).* With them, the psychological implications which condition the rapport between victim and executioner gradually surfaced. As a result, Salome differed only slightly from Judith, triumphing over Holopherne like David over Goliath. A certain form of masculine masochism, allied to the terror of castration, already lay with the severed head upon the silver platter. However, it is necessary to wait for the decadent era to dawn before the image becomes a myth, that haunts the fin de siècle artistic consciousness like a watermark. It is to **Gustave Moreau** *(cat. 49)* that we owe Symbolism's most powerful image, from which the movement, still searching for its identity, was to derive its raison d'être and thrive ; and which was propagated in several different versions by the private painter, forming a real *series* on the **Apparition** theme.

Gustave Moreau's essential contribution to the myth is that the decapitated head is surrounded by a halo of light, emphasizing the awful levitation that takes place in the heavy atmosphere : from this point on, the hallucinatory confrontation can begin between Salome and the bleeding head, horrified at hearing its own interior monologue :

Fig. 50
Titian : Salome (1515)

Fig. 51
Francesco del Cairo : Herodias (c. 1638)

Cat. 49
Moreau: The Apparition

" And my head rises
Watchful alone... "
            (Mallarmé)

It therefore comes as no surprise that Huysmans places this monumental water-color in des Esseintes' revered art collection. " ...The Saint's decapitated head had left the platter where it lay on the flagstones, the eyes staring out from the livid face, the colorless lips parted, the crimson neck dripping tears of blood (...) With a gesture of horror, Salome tries to thrust away the terrifying vision which holds her nailed to the spot, balanced on the tips of her toes, her eyes dilated, her right hand convulsively grabbing at her throat. She is almost naked ; from the emotion of her dance, her veils have fallen away and her brocade robes have slipped to the floor. She is now only clad in wrought metals and translucent gems (...). Never before had an aquarelle attained such an explosion of color, never before had a water-colorist's wretched chemical pigments been able to make paper sparkle so brightly with precious stones, shine so colorfully with sunlight filtered through stained-glass windows, glitter so splendidly with sumptuous garments, or glow so warmly with exquisite flesh-tints. "

Among the cascade of gems and precious hues, Huysmans reveals the archetypal *femme-fatale* who destroys the very object of her passion. **Flaubert** had already given life to Salome's sisters : the Queen of Sheba in *The Temptation of Saint Anthony* (1874) and, to an even greater extent, the chaste, hieratic, and hysterical **Salammbô** (1862, *cat. 59*). In his tale of **Herodias** (1877, *cat. 60*), he

Cat. 55
Rodin: Head of Saint John the Baptist

maintains a dreamy distance which does not focus attention upon the little Salome.

Mallarmé, on the contrary, bestows upon his *Herodiade,* a cold and silver halo where the heroine indulges in morbid fantasies, the product of her lonely agony :

> " I adore the horror of being a virgin and I desire
> To live among the terror of my hair
> To lie upon my bed at night, a reptile
> Undefiled, feeling the useless skin
> The cold sparkle of your faint transparency
> You who are dying, you who burn with chastity
> Sleepless night of icicles and cruel snow ! "

and where the Saint confronts the unspeakable terror of being born again, conscious of his own death : two incommunicable discourses.

The myth is thus established for the years to come, and only knows variations around its hardened core *(cat. 55).*

Jules Laforgue's *Legendary Moralities,* (1886) present a variation on caricature. Salome obtains nothing from her attempts to arouse the severed head, and in her fury, throws it in to the sea, at which point, losing her balance, she joins the head in its fall.

A dramatic variant appears with **Oscar Wilde** (1890, *cat. 63*). It has one act, in unembellished French, the language as measured as it is troubling, and owing

Cat. 62
Wilde : Salomé, illustrations by Beardsley

much to Maeterlinck : " Something terrible will happen ! "; " I have kissed thy mouth, Jokanaan "... As much as Wilde caricatures the vileness of Herodiade, he amplifies the cowardly, lustful, and tormented figure of Herod. No longer is Salome's unleashed sensuality expressed through understatement. At the climax of her erotic paroxysm, while prolongedly kissing the bleeding mouth, Salome understands that her desire, unnamed up to then owing to the innocence of her youth, was merely a quest for absolute purity, an attempt to communicate with the essence of the being that escapes identification : " Had you looked upon me, you would have loved me. And the mystery of love is greater than the mystery of death."

Richard Strauss (*cat. 51, fig. 52*), shortening the length and affectation of the text, in 1906 composed one of the most volcanic operas ever written, with music that constantly gravitates towards the orgasmic. The orchestration, which becomes a torrent of lava or sulphurous vapors, embodies a damp and choking decor. The characters give ear to nothing but their own pulse in an atmosphere that is as thick and opaque as blood. A dense network of leitmotifs evokes the locations of the drama without setting them spatially. All is perceived through the hysteria of Salome : the moon has the chalky pallor of her face, the air vibrates to the rhythm of her heart's palpitations, and her languor is tropical.

" The phosphorescence of putrescence ", proclaimed by Baudelaire is thus achieved by Strauss. His Salome fully attains the paradigmatic image of the female praying mantis, satisfied after the possession of her prey. Her appearance strangely coincides with the twilight of opera. Her natural sisters, Elektra, Turandot, and Lulu, all female devastators, consecrate the death of this genre more profoundly, as if they embodied its inevitable fulfillment and explosion.

Compared to these summits, Massenet's *Herodiade* (1881) can only be a poor contender. Whereas, *The Tragedy of Salome,* by Florent Schmitt (1907), from a poem by Robert d'Humières, is situated halfway between Dukas and Ravel, and develops a harmonic texture of rare luxuriance.

Few painters of the Symbolist movement returned to the Salome theme: Lévy-Dhurmer, Beardsley, Klimt and many unknown painters who dealt in Orientalism ; but throughout, fragments of the myth established by Moreau are to be found : levitating heads by Odilon Redon, provocative Madonnas by Edvard Munch, perverse temptresses by Franz von Stück, and enigmatic *sphinxes* by Fernand Khnopff. They permeated Symbolism so thoroughly, that not much of the original model remained. If there was anything at all, it was but a slight suggestion, a vague memory, a superimposition of analogies.

This is to be seen in the work of two American photographers from the beginning of the century. In **The Kiss, Clarence White** (1904, *Cat. 58*) shows a young woman bestowing a kiss upon a young girl in a very pictorialist and cozy atmosphere. The general effect evokes Beardsley's *Salome,* caressing the head of St. John, but the Pre-Raphaelite references are even more apparent, especially an allusion to Millais's *The Return of the Dove to the Ark* (1851, *fig. 53*), and Windus' *Too Late* (1857-58. *fig. 54*).

Cat. 51
Tilke : Poster for Strauss' *Salome*

Fig. 52
Caricature of Richard Strauss
(1911)

Cat. 58
White: The Kiss

Fig. 53
Millais: The Return of the Dove to the Ark
(1851)

Fig. 54
Windus: Too Late (1857-8)

Cat. 57
Seeley: The Brass Bowl

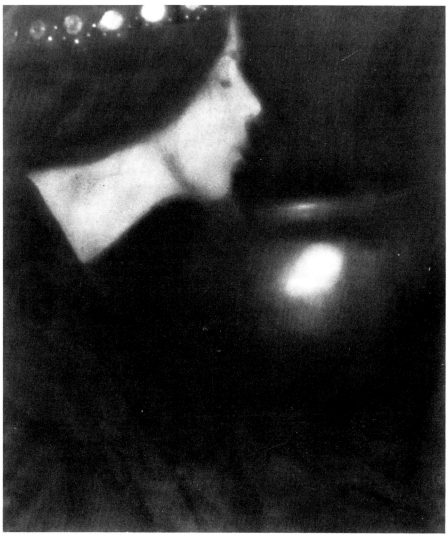

Georges Seeley, friend of the latter and also gravitating about *Camera Work,* proposed à Titianesque Salome in **The Brass Bowl** (1905, *cat. 57*). A vase has replaced the severed head, and the image is considerably less dramatic; it has become a very aesthetic *icon of transition,* in which the poetic inertia entraps the myth.

Now far from its point of departure, the drift, the pullulation of symbolist imagery is no longer controllable; the walls of the sphere have been so dilated that its own center has disappeared.

Fig. 55
Debussy: Prélude à l'après-midi d'un faune

The Dream in its Domain

" Did I love a dream ? " asks Mallarmé's Faun. Under the blistering mid-day sun, the doubt of the oneiric division fills him with languor. To pursue the nymphs is to name them, to " perpetuate " them, only to grasp their shadows. The ascending hold of sleep in this way becomes the mandatory environment for the idea's fertility.

Does this mean that the close of Romanticism had to be attained for the dream to find its place? Ever since the grim and hallucinatory works of Blake and Füssli *(fig. 56)*, to which it is necessary to add the strand of thought that belongs to Hölderlin and Novalis, Romanticism had been thoroughly convinced of the central position occupied by the dream in the origins of the creative process. If it is necessary to look for earlier proofs we could return to Artemidorus, whose *Onirokritika* attempted the first thorough interpretation of the dream.

With Symbolism, the dream became the inevitable path, the very condition of creative activity. The role of Edgar Allan Poe was critical in the abandoning of all the satanic and flamboyant aspects which had played such an important part in the success of Gothic Romanticism, and made inevitable the irruption of the fantastic dimension within the field of reality. Significantly, in Poe, Henry James, Maupassant, or Wilde, the devil is merely a grotesque puppet, and ghosts are treated with irony.

Interest shifted to a study of suggestion, of cerebral depression, where the morbid chimera that gathered in the new imagery sought escape. With the installation of a decadent culture, the fantastic did not lead to a disintegration of reality; instead, it originated in the clinical observation of *mental agony* experienced by the hyper-sensitive hero, and in the effervescent progression of the symptoms of his condition. The decor of modernity only heightened the fear, matching its own trivial and superficial coherance against the much crueller coherance of delirium. The rose glittering in the dark is a sick rose, gnawed from the interior, much as Blake imagined it.

Fig. 56
Füssli: The Nightmare (1781)

Fig. 57
Khnopff: "I lock my door upon myself" (1891)

Fig. 58
Redon: The Prisoner (c. 1880)

Fig. 59
Redon: Within the Dream: *Vision* (1879)

Fig. 60
Redon: To Edgar Poe, *A Mask Rings the Funeral Bell* (1882)

For he who knows how to remain in the transient state between sleeping and waking, the dream can be transcribed in terms of memory, understood here as the sphere of images buried in the past. In Poe, as in Swinburne, or Mallarmé, memory strengthens absence, and the consciousness which palpitates at a different rhythm during sleep has only to measure the volume of space which encloses it. This explains the sensation of claustrophobia to be found in numerous Symbolist works, where everything is suffocated, even the echo.

The Symbolist decor often called for stagnant waters, crystalline prisons, spiralling movements, aquatic dying cities, and above all, artificial reproduction of reality that is like a challenge to the Creator's work; as des Esseintes says " ... No waterfall that cannot be imitated by hydraulics, no rock that cannot be rendered in cardboard. " Through this progressive vampirization, the attempt to escape from the dream's enchanted circle is rendered hopeless.

Consequently, the dream is all but an evasion, as it was conceived by the Romantics. It is an imperative invitation to *search within one's self*. It becomes a recess in dense forests where no sunlight penetrates, the air is motionless, and the waters have ceased to run. Long before Freud published *The Interpretation of Dreams* (1900), the Symbolists had considered the parallel life of the unconscious as something already acquired. But for the founder of psychoanalysis, the dream was above all the disguised wish-fulfillment of a repressed desire : " The process which in collaboration with censorship is performed by dream work in translating the latent content into the manifest content is called *wish fulfillment*. It consists of a particular treatment of preconcious thought material in which these processes are *condensed,* their psychic accents are *displaced* and transposed into visual *dramatized* images, to be completed by the *secondary process* of waking thought which renders all incomprehensible. "

Freud did not clearly define the notion of symbols, which he often confused with substitution, representation, or allusion.

Fig. 61
Kubin: The Other Side (1908)

Whereas, for the Symbolists, this was an active process which accomplished, in the dream's field of vision, the clandestine work of regenerating the subconscious. Thoughts which were elaborated during the oneiric process were capable of sailing far beyond natural limits, beyond speech and representation. For this reason oneiric activity became the favored terrain of creative exaltation : painting and literature bathed in the dream, amidst a climate of drug addiction (widespread in very refined circles) that was rendered even more propitious to visions. With novelists as bleak as Barbey d'Aurevilly or Villiers de l'Isle-Adam, the narrative distance has the opacity of a troubled dream. In Henry James's *The Turn of the Screw* (1898), the ghosts that haunt the manor house are perhaps a mere result of the hysteria that gradually takes hold of the children's governess. In Alfred Kubin's novel *The Other Side* (1908, *fig. 61*) the obsession with confinement in Pearl's Empire anticipates Kafka's *Castle,* and has all the viscosity of a long nightmare. The characters in Maeterlinck's plays from *Princess Maleine* (1890) to *Tintagiles' Death* (1894) are, according to their creator, puppets, " looking like slightly deaf sleepwalkers, constantly torn from a painful dream. "

Reaching an even more febrile stage, the familiarity of the dream becomes a permanent catharsis. Rimbaud's *Illuminations* (1886) succeed better than any other in translating the Dionysian ecstasy of destructive creation :

" A prince was vexed for having only excelled in the perfection of vulgar extravagancies. (...)
All the women that he had known were murdered. What havoc in beauty's garden ! When beneath the sword, they gave him their blessing. He didn't ask for any replacements — The women reappeared.
He killed all who followed him, his hunting and drinking companions — And yet they continued to follow him.
He amused himself by slitting the throats of his rare animals. He burned his palaces.
He flung himself upon the people and cut them to pieces — The crowd, the golden roof tops, the beautiful beasts still existed.
Can one achieve ecstasy by destruction, become younger through cruelty ! "

No one can ignore that Symbolism used a mythology that had already existed for centuries. It dealt mostly with a diurnal transcription of immaterial impulses, embodied with the risk of becoming unnatural. Certain artists, nevertheless, succeeded in approaching the core of the dream without any mythological medley, almost achieving the evocation of the inexpressible.

Odilon Redon, among them, seemed as fully conscious as Maeterlinck that " we live next to our real lives. " From the agony of the first *black* works, *(In my Dream* (1879), *Hommage to Edgar A. Poe* (1882), and *Hommage to Goya* (1885), up to the chromatic jubilation of his later pastels, he appeared to be totally absorbed by an interior vision. " In art, all is accomplished by docile submission to the

Cat. 52
Redon: Closed Eyes

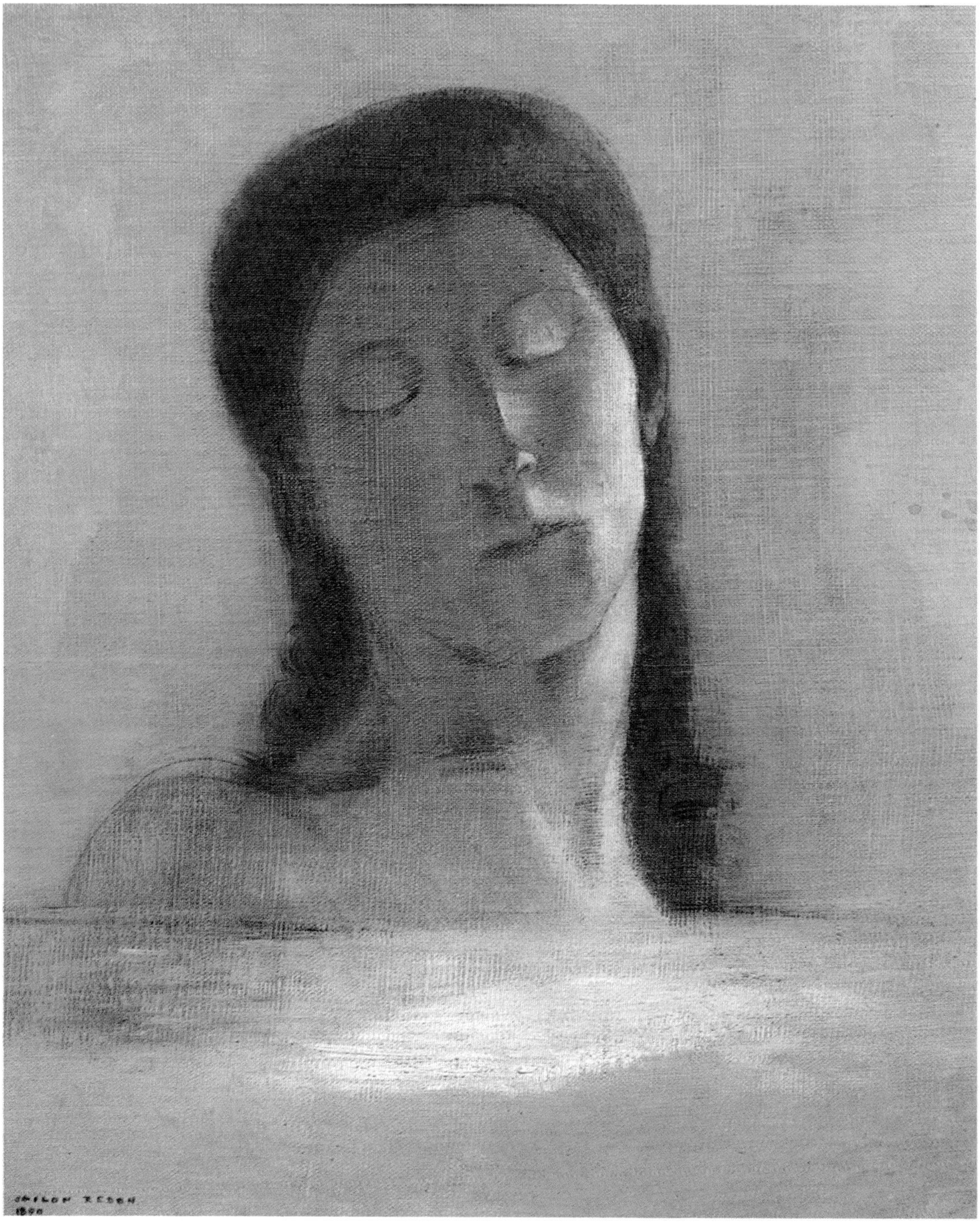

Cat. 50
Spilliaert: Moonlight and Lights

unconscious, " Redon confides in his collection of thoughts significantly entitled *To Myself.* In the delicately bluish atmosphere of **With Closed Eyes** (1890, *cat. 52),* he gives this head the serene inclination of Michelangelo's *Dying Slave.* " Slave's slumber awakening our dignity ". Emerging from the waters of the unconscious, the face appears to be completely occupied by an interior meditation that is strong enough to set the chaos of the world in order. This is an ultimate expression of the being thinking of itself as the universe's echo, rather in the manner of " I celebrate Myself ", by Walt Whitman, opening the torrent of images in *Leaves of Grass* (1855), or as in *Transcendance* (1908) by Stefan George :

" ... I lose myself in sonorities,
I am but the echo of God's voice. "

Answering Rimbaud's " *I* is someone else ", the entire world is here reflected in *me* : transcending matter and memory in a vanishing look. The consciousness observing itself dreaming, endeavors to suspend its immobile flight, and awaken to truth. As Edgar A. Poe stated, " We are on the verge of awakening when we dream that we are dreaming. "

On the other hand, the environment can *return* fragments of the image of the self ; but in this case it is an organized environment, full of meaning, brought to light by a look that travels through time. Rilke gave it ideal expression in *The Death of the Poet* :

" Those who saw him live, ignored
To what extent he was on with All :
Because these ravines, these prairies,
And these waters, *were* his face. "

Deeply influenced by Maeterlinck's poetry, the Belgian **Léon Spilliaert,** an enthusiast of Ostend, like Ensor, made this sea resort a kind of mirror of his inner world, with its naked and obsessive geometry that distills an incommunicable sense of solitude. **Moonlight and Lights** (1909, *cat. 50),* is one of the rare views of the Ostend Casino where the sea is abolished by the delirious framing of the subject. The royal gallery is thrust to the side, as though seen through a *fish-eye* lens, to allow the heavy meanderings of the black and grey sky to triumph, seeming, to " weigh down like a lid " (Baudelaire) despite the transparency of the diluted tints. " The stormy paradise collapses. " A sort of opium induced dream, this vision reminds one of the glaucous labyrinths in Rodenbach's Bruges-la-Morte (1892, *fig. 62*), or of certain nocturnal and marine exaltations in Rimbaud's *A Season in Hell* (1875) : " Let the towns kindle in the night ; my day is over. I'm leaving Europe. The sea air shall burn my lungs (...) Now I am cursed, horrified by my country. The best thing is a good drunken sleep on the sea shore. " The gaslights of the embankment silently shatter like so many moons, denoucing the evil ascendancy of the pale planet upon the helpless human will.

Closely related at first glance, is the small **Moonlight** by **Vallotton** (1895), through whose sharp Japanese line an even more total absence is suggested ;. a

Fig. 62
W. Degouve de Nuncques : The Night in Brugges (1897)

Cat. 53
Vallotton : Moonlight

Cat. 54
Lacombe: Existence

human absence, as well as an absence of all vibration; a kind of metamorphosis into mineral consciousness, like that of a lunar desert. The strange symmetry due to the reflection in the water suggests the idea of two hemispheres united by a total void. There is an absolute silence. Since the landscape is now just an inward looking sign, the mind is able to observe itself from outside its biological and intellectual life and move freely in the most confined spaces where dizziness spreads its wings.

The last stage of oneiric activity is the organic transcription of the dreamt concept, extremely rare, but particularly successful in George **Lacombe's Existence** (cat. 54). Both a painter and sculptor, he was introduced to the *Nabi* circle by Sérusier sometime in 1892. He seemed, more than the others, to lean toward esoterism and appeared to take the word *Nabi* (prophet) literally while sculpting the four wood panels for a bed (1894-96). They represent *Conception, Birth* and *Death*. The head board is entitled " Existence " , long referred to as *The Dream* due to its hermetic inspiration. Despite references to Maori sculpture or to the more contemporary work of Gauguin, nothing up to this point had resembled this incredible intertwining receptacle of the mysteries of existence.

The two lovers are united in one monumental face by the contracting snake-like spirals that symbolize a perpetual renewal of the inextinguishable forces governing the universe. A double pentacle allows spermatozoides to shoot forth while a large lanceolated leaf symbolizes the feminine sexual organs.

Rarely had the mysterious essence of life's gift been distilled to such an extent. Without a doubt, the influence of Edouard Shuré's *Grands Initiés* hovers over the work. But above all, Lacombe had known where to find, at the frontiers of abstraction, a sense of pre-Christian sacredness, of revelations from before the dawn, an oneiric ataraxia, a communion, intuitive and misty, with the divine mysteries, as they might have been expressed by Sapho in the *Odes* :

" Tonight, I spoke at length in my dream with Aphrodite. "

Drawings and Watercolors

Fantin-Latour Henri (1836-1904), French

47 *Isolde in the Tower*
(Isolde à la Tour)
(28.3 × 25.5 cm)
RF 15650

48 *Siegfried and the Rhine Maidens*
(Siegfried et les filles du Rhin)
(31.2 × 24.5 cm)
RF 12838

Moreau Gustave (1826-1898), French

49 *The Apparition,* 1875
(L'Apparition)
Aquarelle (106 × 72.2 cm)
Signed bottom left in gold : *Gustave Moreau*
Given by the artist to the Luxembourg Museum in 1898
RF 2130

Spilliaert Léon (1881-1946), Belgian

50 *Moonlight and Lights,* 1909
(Clair de lune et Lumières)
China ink wash and pastel
(65 × 50 cm)
Signed bottom right: L. Spilliaert
Gift of Mme Madeleine Spilliaert, daughter of the artist, 1981
RF 38835

Tilke Max, (1869- ?) German

51 *Poster for Strauss' Salome,* 1910
(77 × 56 cm)
Paris, Opera Library

Painting

Redon Odilon (1844-1916), French

52 *Closed Eyes,* 1890
(Les Yeux Clos)
Oil on canvas (44 × 36 cm)
Signed and dated bottom left : *Odilon Redon, 1890*
Acquired for the Musée du Luxembourg, 1904
RF 2791

Vallotton Félix (1865-1925), Swiss

53 *Moonlight,* 1895
(Clair de lune)
Oil on canvas (27 × 41 cm)
Signed and dated bottom right : *F. Vallotton 1895*
Acquired in 1979
RF 1979-60

Sculpture

Lacombe George (1868-1916), French

54 *Existence,* 1892
(L'Existence)
Wood panel (68.5 × 141.5 × 6 cm)
Acquired from Mrs. Lacombe in 1956
RF 3221

Rodin Auguste (1840-1917), French

55 *Head of Saint John the Baptist*
(Tête coupée de St Jean Baptiste)
Bronze (21 × 41 × 27 cm)
Lux 163
Paris, Musée Rodin

Troubetzkoy Prince Paul (1866-1938), Russian

56 *Robert de Montesquiou,* 1907
Bronze (56 × 62 × 56.5 cm)
Signed and dated: *Paul Troubetzkoy,
Paris 1907:* above impression
CIRE / C. VALSUANI / PERDUE
Acquired at Public Auction, 1980
RF 3476

Photography

Seeley George-Henry (1880-1955), American

57 *The Brass Bowl,* 1905
Platinum print
(35 × 29 cm)
Acquired in Washington in 1984
PHO 1984-56

White Clarence-Hudson (1871-1925), American

58 *The Kiss,* 1904
    Platinum print
    (24.7 × 14.8 cm)
    Gift of the C.D.F. Chimie-Terpolymères Company 1985
    PHO 1985-357

Books

Flaubert Gustave (1821-1878), French

59 *Salammbô,* Paris 1900
    Illustrations by Rochegrosse

60 *Hérodias,* London, 1901
    Illustrations by Lucien Pissarro

Huysmans Joris-Karl (1848-1907), French

61 *Against Nature,* Paris 1903
    (A Rebours)
    Illustrations by Lepère

Wilde Oscar (1854-1900), English

62 *Salomé,* Paris 1907
    Illustrations by Beardsley

The above books have been lent by the *Paris National Library*

Model

Chapcron Philippe-Marie (1823-1907), French

63 Model for Wagner's *Tannhäuser*
    Replica of the 1845 stage-setting
    (22.5 × 31.3 cm)
    Paris, Opera Library

From Stage Performance to Representation

Dante, Shakespeare, Goethe

To represent is both to put something onto a stage and to exhibit it to the public. A conflict of principles arises between an approach claiming to reproduce plain reality and that which claims to organize it into a collection of recognizable signs. In the Romantic mentality, this dichotomy was resolved through an osmosis where the various visual fine arts reflected the new tensions inspired by a different kind of theater. This projected Shakespeare into the foreground of Romantic thought. Of course, the discovery of Shakespeare in France did not date from 1830; Voltaire had already incorporated large excerpts from Shakespeare in his classically structured tragedies, but the Romantic generation made him their figurehead. By means of new publications and translations, musicians, poets, painters and men of the stage discovered a dramatic language which reflected a world at the peak of its ambiguity and diversity: in this world the grotesque sounded metaphysical, the noblest expectations were seen to be consecrated to ridiculous results, solitude was incommunicable and passion was atrocious. "Fair is foul and foul is fair".

Shakespeare was perceived as the beacon of a general reversal of values, the same reversal that Romanticism was aiming to accomplish. Above all, he offered a theatrical model which never took into account the three-unit rule (time, space and action) of classical French theater. On the contrary, he activated historical time and stressed it in a completely disseminated theatrical space.

To the Shakespearian imagery which contaminates the entire romantic culture, one must add the imagery of Faust. In *Faust* by Goethe (1776-1826, *fig. 65*), a dramatic narrative of an expressly hybrid sort, philosophical speculation, absolute desire, impotency of will-power and grimacing horror become magnified and sulphurous. The character of Faust can be interpreted as a remarkable abbreviation of the 19th century artist's continual and desperate search for change, where movement in time and space expresses the quest for a renewal of vision. Here, he reveals his fraternity with the hero of the *Divine Comedy,* another

Fig. 63
Delacroix: The Death of Ophelia
(1844)

Fig. 64
Chassériau: Macbeth and the Witches
(1855)

Fig. 65
Tissot: The Encounter of Faust and Marguerite
(1860)

observer of mysteries in a world turned upside down, a docile instrument at the hands of his guide. Even the dream-like transitions that bind the episodes of the Faustian race to the abyss, echo with the swoonings of Dante from one circle of hell to the next. From this mere detail, insignificant at first glance, we have the key to a theatrical and visual art which depends upon a magical adhesion to the illusion of reality.

It is therefore no coincidence that Dante, Goethe and Shakespeare form the fundamental referential triad of the great Romantics, such as Delacroix the illustrator of both *Faust* and *Hamlet,* or as Berlioz, whose musical works such as *Lelio,* The *Damnation of Faust* and *Romeo and Juliet* contain at the same time dramatic legend, interior monologue, oratorio and free improvisation. With the dissolution of the strictly partitioned genre a new way of sectioning drama came into focus and consequently a new way of representing it appeared on canvas. The language itself reflected this mutation : in French and Italian, " tableau " and " quadro " replaced the habitual word for *scene* during the Romantic era.

Chassériau *(cat. 65),* an ardent reader of Shakespeare, dedicated numerous paintings to the tragedies, particularly to *Othello* and *Macbeth.* The sketch for **Romeo and Juliet** (1850) represents the denouement of the famous tragedy : like Paolo and Francesca in *The Divine Comedy,* the two lovers join together for a last mortal embrace. Far from the Neo-Raphaelite style of Ary Sheffer, Chassériau sketches the scene with a very nervous brush stroke ; a few strokes suffice to evoke the heavy pillars and the recumbent figure on the tomb. The dominance of ochre and brown is illuminated by hints of carmine and white on the bodies of the two young people, but the general effect remains very fluid and only the over-turned cup in the foreground glows more clearly. Not only does the emotion of Delacroix show through in this scene numbed by the despondency of death, but also some of Daumier's allusive style.

Shakespeare's theater and the texts which can be associated with it, particularly those of Victor Hugo and Schiller, introduced the pursuit of historical credibility in stage production allied to a conception of history that was deeply dramatic. In the foreword to his play, *Cromwell* (1827), Hugo defines the principles which were to govern the stage for half a century :

" We are currently beginning to understand that exact location is one of the primary elements of reality. The personalities speaking or acting are not the only elements that engrave a truthful print of the deeds upon the spectator's mind. The site where the catastrophe takes place become its terrible and inseparable witness ; and the absence of this sort of mute personnage would banish the greatest scenes of history from the drama. Would the poet dare murder Rizzio elsewhere than in the chamber of Mary Stuart ?, stab Henry IV elsewhere than the Rue de la Ferronnerie, completely obstructed by wheel-barrows and coaches ?, burn Joan of Arc elsewhere than the Old Market Place ?, hasten the Duc de Guise elsewhere than to the Castle of Blois, where his ambition leads him to incite the mobs ?, behead Charles I or

Louis XVI elsewhere than in the sinister sites where we can see Whitehall and the Tuileries as though the scaffold were a pendant upon their palaces?"

This very particular theatrical prism refracted a way of looking at history which favored individual psychology, court plots, corruption by power and the solitude of the powerful. In painting, as in the theater the spotlight was fixed on the culminating moments of dramatic intensity: Mary Stuart's last moments, the waiting of Edward's offspring in the tower, Joan of Arc in prison — "grand dramatic moments" which were the delight of a painter like Paul Delaroche (fig. 66), as well as his cornucopia.

"Everything transient was but an appearance", claims the luminous conclusion in Faust. In fact, this kind of painting offers the feeling of immediacy combined with duration. A dense aggregation of meaning in a single gesture or glance implies the suspended development of an action that closes in on itself. From these few hints, a person with little cultural background is able to perceive the antecedents and the consequences, thus reconstructing the dramatic episode as a whole. The pleasure of the image is then more literary than visual. This kind of painting which outlives its denouement aggregates a series of moments in the process of becoming eternal. History is in this way capable of being restored into slices of eternity.

Fig. 66
Delaroche: Edward's Children (1830)

Fig. 67
Tissot: The Prodigal Son (1862)

History and Illusion

Romanticism consecrated a moment in Western culture where the desire to possess the world was no longer founded on symbolic discourse, but on a panoramic fullness of vision. In this way, theater lent support to painting. Three columns no longer sufficed to embody the Palace of Nero as they had in the time of Racine's tragedies. The development of means of communication, the multiplication of travel accounts, the constantly improved knowledge of history by means of archeology affected the public so that it was no longer satisfied by an allegorical evocation of a locality and of the described epoch, but demanded a representation, a faithful reconstruction of reality. Little did it matter that the Elizabethans had been pleased with simple panels on which the location of drama was named, or if the continual changing of the stage scenery upset the rhythm and dramatic unity of the Romantic theater. The set decorators who displayed real artistic talent, such as Ciceri in Paris and Sanquirico at La Scala in Milan, vied in invention and erudition with the painters. Théophile Gautier, for whom the visual arts were a spectacle and theater a visual pleasure, noted in 1866: " To meet the unforeseen demands of the authors, one must know every land, epoch and style completely; one must know geology, the flora and the architecture of the four corners of the earth and even that is not cnough... an author may write at the beginning of an act 'this scene takes place in Byzantium', and the artist quickly builds a Byzantine

palace with semi-circular arches, a dome, porphyritic columns, mosaics with a golden background to which the architect of Justinian I, Arthemius of Tralles, would find no reproach".

The Romantic theater loved to associate real furnishings with flat painted canvas scenery, a vulgar artifice in which the illusionistic effect was only guaranteed by means of dimming the footlights. Skilled stage-hands helped the stage designer accomplish the excesses of the Baroque stage by rendering the spectacular effects more and more naturalistic : floods, volcanic eruptions, fires, landslides, etc. As the theater director stated in the prologue to *Faust* :

" Offer a universe to the suprised spectators...
Why do they come ? To see, to see at any cost.
Know then how to capture their esteem,
And for them you will be the ultimate poet ".

The stage in this way united the tragic action with the panoramic yearning enchantment of Daguerre's "diorama" which drew the appreciative public eager to see the reconstructed landscapes. The world of performance, taken in its most picturesque and most pathetic periphery, in other words one that was immediately recognizable, induced a more rapid research, not only by the use of photography, but also through the impoverishment of symbolic imagination ; the risk often being a desire to show all while leaving as little as possible to conjecture.

The return in force of neo-classicism with Thomas Couture, and especially Gérôme (his *Cock-fight* dates from 1846) did not alter the problem. Greco-Roman antiquity lost its dimension of idealism to become a mere pretext, a no less noble attire, because it had received the Academy's blessing. Castagnary said of Gérôme, who on request changed his rhetor's costume to that of a caravaneer, " He dresses his figures like a costume designer ; he places them as if they were on stage ". (Salon of 1863)

The exalting effects of the city's perspective had already been known for quite some time. From Piero della Francesca to Poussin and later David, the planned insertion of protagonists and crowd in a succession of perfect volumes strengthened the visual expression of a philosophic ideal. In the middle of the 19th century it became a question of competing with the architectural surveys in which the precision, the morbid meticulousness of detail were savored by a public who used them to confirm their well-bred erudition. Painting, like theater, functioned as a museum.

No " genre " escaped this standardization. Even the Orientalist paintings were treated as stage sets : in the foreground, an anonymous crowd in folkloric costume, or a ruin and palm trees in the shade which cuts the middle ground flooded by sunlight where the principal subject stands, perhaps a town, an arab camping ground, a hunting scene, a monastery, while in the background the desert and the sky reunite in a bluish mist. It comes as no surprise then, that this

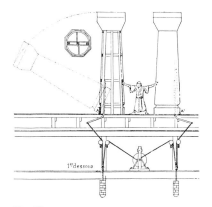

Fig. 68
Stage setting for *Samson et Dalila*
by Saint-Saëns

Fig. 69
Daumier : The Mother of Love

Fig. 70
Gérôme : The Death of Ceasar (1860-67)

Cat. 74
Vallou de Villeneuve : The Actress Rachel

painting, centered on its stage setting and " performing " desperately clings to a perspective inherited from the Italian Renaissance, which it considers to be the only cradle of truth ; whereas, in reality, it is only a coded illusion, an abstraction of the retina alone, which is mechanically conditioned. The demand for a historic likelihood, both topographical and psychological, was similarly transformed in painting into a demand for spatial and pathological theatrics.

Delaunay's " The Plague in Rome " (1869, *cat. 67*), which was famous in its day, is a good example of this trend. During his stay in Rome he discovered in the church of St. Peter in Chains a fresco narrating the plague of 680 (the work of an assistant of Cosimo Rosselli, according to Berenson), with an angel inciting a demon to knock on the doors of the condemned, that illustrates a passage from *The Golden Legend* (c 1264) by Jacopo da Voragine : " And then appeared in sight a good angel who ordered the bad angel, armed with a spear, to strike the dwellings, and as many times as a home was struck there were to be that many deaths ". The numerous preliminary drawings which succeed one another from

Cat. 67
Delaunay: The Plague in Rome

Cat. 68
Laurens: The Excommunication of Robert the Pious

1857 on inform us of the evolution of the placement of elements in the painting. In the first versions, the angel and the vengeful demon are distinctly separated; subsequenty they become a single expanding triangular form, a sort of swooning fever cast upon a bluish night where all life comes to a standstill. Edmond About, a celebrated journalist and sometime art critic, had been impressed by this " heavy and suffocating atmosphere in which vileness is diffused in the air ". The monuments seem to have been gathered here specially for the occasion : the stairs of the Ara Cœli, the tower of Milices, the statue of Marc-Aurele (which looks more like the Venitian Colleone by Verrocchio), are organized to carefully partition the space, at the risk of making it appear a bit skimpy, like the flats, the practicables and the backdrops used on the stage. As with the theater, the problematical succession of " scenes " dissolves into an advantageous obscurity, where the figures stricken by the plague consolidate to favor the triumph of emptiness in the center of the composition.

Even more celebrated is **J.P. Laurens's " Excommunication of Robert-the-Pious "** (1875, *cat. 68*), an essential icon of scholarly handbooks for more than half a century. Last among the great historical painters at the end of the 19th century, Laurens was himself conscious of the illustrative function of this painting. A profound atheist and humanist, he used his vast erudition to exhume little known episodes which stigmatized the intolerance of the church. Nevertheless, he remained intransigent to the revolutions which agitated the world of art around him. " We repeatedly hear that history has had its day, that in art the subject does not matter, that a market merchant or a beautiful lady in her opera loge are just as interesting and poetic as the historic heroes of France. This is not my opinion [...] do we know whether tomorrow we shall not appear ridiculous ourselves ? " For him, as well as for Jules Michelet, history was a resurrection. King Robert-the-Pious, successor of Hughes Capet, had repudiated his first wife to marry his cousin (four times removed), Berthe de Bourgogne in 989, whom he dearly loved. Pope George V reasoned on this argument to demand the separation of the couple, and presented with the determined refusal of Robert, excommunicated him as well as the entire kingdom. Added to the collective fears that shook Europe at the end of the First Millennium, the excommunication proved to be an effective arm — abandoned by all, the King was forced to separate from Berthe in the year 1001.

Fig. 71
Laurens: The Men of the Inquisition (1882)

Laurens could have chosen the moment when the Papal nuncio executes the sentence in the presence of the court; he preferred to show the bareness of the room that the cardinals have just left. The King and Queen remain cowering and prostrate in the large chamber where the candle of excommunication still smokes. The oblique vanishing lines converge towards the obscured door that has swallowed the prelates, accentuating the couple's solitude and desolation. The interest of this scene resides mostly in its refusal of gesture, its restraint and lack of demonstrative expression.

Once again, as in the *Plague in Rome,* the void is the composition's real protagonist; the void that betrays so well the theatrical substance of this sort of

Cat. 79
Frémiet: Costumes for Mermet's *Joan of Arc* (1876)

Fig. 72
L. Alma-Tadema: Sappho (1881)

painting, from which emanates an indubitable nostalgic charm, as well as a total lack of significant autonomy. The suspension of movement, the unappeased tension to conquer the space, that which can only really be accomplished in the theater or even more so in the opera, clearly marks the impassable limits of this type of art, its structural impotency to do anything else but tell a story; especially if it is one from History.

Beside Laurens' notable success a series of every day works poured forth from the brushes of artists like Detaille, Maignan, Cormon, or the eternal Gérôme for whom inspiration remained a sordid combination of accessories borrowed from second-hand clothiers. An artist like **Emmanuel Frémiet** drew the costumes for Mermet's opera **Joan of Arc** *(cat. 79)* performed at the Paris Opera in 1876; Meissonier did not hesitate to do the same for other productions. Their paintings become standardized as quickly as the representations in which they participated. It is quite revealing that the costumes conceived by Gustave Moreau for Gounod's *Sapho* (1884) remained in their preliminary stages. In the work of successful painters such as Lawrence Alma-Tadema *(fig. 72),* one clearly recognizes his contemporaries with their bourgeois look " à la Tissot " disguised

Cat. 72
Mercié: David

as ancient Athenians or Romans in decors that announce the future colossal productions of Hollywood. His proconsuls unfailingly look like stock-brokers, his bacchants agitate like suffragettes and his bathers discover Victorian lasciviousness.

In the same way, sculpture has difficulty in avoiding the ostentatious gesture and the unremitting unfurling of scenes stolen from Ovid, Plutarch or Livy, like actors who cannot abandon a tendency to station themselves on stage in idealized poses. Exploiting a slightly breathless biblical vein is **Mercié's " David "** (1872, *cat. 72*) which stands as a brilliant exception. The young hero is shown only after his task has been accomplished, with one foot crushing the severed head of Goliath while he puts his sword back in its sheath. No gesture could be simpler, but it is one to which the sculptor confers both amplitude and restraint : a halo of eternity seems to spread around the body.

The success of this statue at the Salon was indescribable. A discreet allusion to the belittled France, who would one day take her revenge on the Prussian Goliath may have been perceived. The critics, P. Mantz in particular, insisted on the influence of Donatello or Verrocchio, especially for the delicate curve, almost oriental in its bearing.

Towards Cinema ?

Fig. 73
Rejlander: The Two Ways of Life (1857)

Fig. 74
Robinson: Fading Away (1858)

It is well known that photography, rather than the traditional arts, was the catalyst of direct experience in the plastic arts. Amidst the suspicion which surrounded it, because of its industrial origin, this evolving language borrowed its *raison d'être* from the other more experienced languages. The " pictorialist" tendency of photography began very early. Rejlander's, in his *Two Ways of Life* (1857, *fig. 73*), elaborated a sort of kitsch *School of Athens,* where Good (Devotion, Chastity, Work) was confronted with Bad (Desire, Cupidity, Luxury). To express his ideas, he superimposed nearly thirty negatives which gave a strange thickness to the depth of field. Even more scenographic is H. Peach Robinson's *Fading Away* (1858, *fig. 74*), which shows the agony of a dying youth in a very austere atmosphere where the sophistication of the natural image is pushed to its limits. One feels that all has been meticulously prepared, designed, juxtaposed, installed and set into a somewhat mawkish poem. In his treatise *Pictorial Effect in Photography* (1869), Robinson states, " one must at all costs reject disgraceful forms and give picturesqueness to that which has none ".

Robinson condescendingly considered the work of **Julia Margaret Cameron** " poorly defined ". The photographs illustrating *Tennyson's* **Idylls of the Kings** (1875) breathe a far greater spontaneity. One can not imagine more scenographic " tableaux vivants " than those executed at the request of the poet and interpreted by friends, domestics and the village people who lived around the home of Cameron on the Isle of Wight. This small parish theater group would

Cat. 73 a
Cameron: *The Beguiling of Merlin*

Cat. 73 b
Cameron: *The Parting of Lancelot and Guenevere*

Cat. 73 c
Cameron: *The Passing of Arthur*

Cat. 73 d
Cameron: *Like a Shatter'd Column Lay the King*

pose for hours before her camera which was already technically out-dated. The incomparable strength of her art comes precisely from her total lack of prejudice, from the disconcertingly pure amazement at the world itself that she expresses with total liberty, and which her evident permeability to the Pre-Raphaelite climate does not compromise.

" I had no idea where to put my ' black box ', how to frame my model ", she confided later. In her *Parting of Lancelot and Guenevere (cat. 73 b)*, she avoids cluttering the image with medieval odds and ends as outlined in the poem, which Hunt or Millais would have adored to decorate. She leaves the two lovers entwined, wearing their poor garments, to accentuate the distress of their separation :

> " And Lancelot promised, but remain'd,
> And still they met and met. "

The maximum of theatrical direction is achieved in the funeral of Arthur : *So like a shatter'd column lay the King (cat. 73 d)*. Against poorly drawn tapestries lightly illuminated by the pallor of a cardboard moon, the funeral barque, too small to contain the virgins who accompany the deceased, moves across the lake made of whitened zones on the zinc-plates ; and yet the errors of manipulation united with the simplicity of the centering reinforces the miraculous aura that surrounds this enthusiast's endeavors — an enthusiast completely devoured by her art. In *The Passing of Arthur (cat. 73 c)*, she succeeds, according to her own words, in rendering " the greatness of the interior being " by closely scrutinizing the king's face, attaining an unprecedented and quite advanced way of centering the image. Meanwhile, *The Beguiling of Merlin (cat. 73 a)*, marvellously interpreted in Burne Jones' painting (1878), remained too close to the obvious theatrical posture.

With these ephemeral works, we have the rare example of an art which proceeds from a very exterior and recognized theatricality, to gradually become impregnated by its own rhythm, through the circular process of a secret maieutic.

As for the Pre-Raphaelites, they resorted to photography very early in the movement. The best known case is that of Rossetti, weaving through the lens his own love affair with Jane Morris, who haunts his later work. But generally speaking, the Pre-Raphaelite compositions are somewhat less theatrical due to a sensibility directed more at the expression of poetic rhythm. It is revealing that **Ford Madox Brown,** when dealing with a myth as dramatic as that of Don Juan, should choose the rather marginal interpretation of Byron's poem. **The finding of Don Juan by Haidee** (1878, *cat. 64*) is the illustration of verses 110-112 of Canto II :

> " And like a wither'd lily, on the land
> His slender frame and pallid aspect lay
> As fair thing as e'er was formed of clay. "

Cat. 64
Brown: The Finding of Don Juan by Haidee

Fig. 75
Delacroix: Don Juan's Shipwreck (1840)

Fig. 76
Viollet-le-Duc: Project for the Paris Opera House (1861)

Abandoning the theme of " dissoluto punito ", Brown resolutely participates in the reversal of conception that runs through the whole of Romanticism. " Our old friend Don Juan " is presented to us as a powerless victim who is constantly endangered by his courage and his anticonformism. He becomes the embodiment of the free being in search of individual achievement. Later in the century, literature and the visual arts were to be subject to monstrous characters such as that of Salome or that of Dorian Gray and their quest for absolute purity, even at the price of destroying those around them who are opposed to it.

In the 19th century, both theater and opera remained at the heart of cultural preoccupations, as is noticable by the importance given to the construction of theatres throughout Europe during this time. The grand architectural event of the Second Empire was the *competition for the design of the* **Paris Opera House** *(cat. 69)* in December 1860. The eclectic-palladian and baroque project presented by **Charles Garnier** was chosen over the more austere project of **A.N. Crépinet** *(cat. 71)* or that of Viollet-le-Duc which was hardly even considered. Immediately the Garnier Palace became the center of the Haussmann's urban system.

On the question of the distribution of interior space, Garnier lent a deaf ear to the innovations defended by Wagner, which were carried out a year after the Paris Opera had been completed in 1876 for the Festspielhaus in Bayreuth. The construction of a semicircular concert hall replaced the tiering of boxes and the

Cat. 69
Crépinet: Project for the New Opera House

Cat. 71
Carpeaux: Bust of Charles Garnier

Cat. 70
Merson: Lady Macbeth Sleep-walking

Fig. 77
Füssli: Lady Macbeth with the Daggers (1812)

Fig. 78
Jarry: King Ubu (1896)

orchestra was located under the stage, a mystical abyss from which sounds emerged without distracting the public concentrated on the visual spectacle. This inaugurated a new type of lyrical drama which played upon the strings of ecstasy and incantation. Th. W. Adorno has demonstrated how the Wagnerian fantasy is a revelation of industrial technology's moment of maximum expansion; to be convincing it requires a state of total abandonment and mental intoxication.

Was traditional drama destined to disappear? Verdi's final operas suffice to prove the contrary: *Otello* (1887) and *Falstaff* (1893) from Shakespeare, far from being the survivors of a outmoded genre, achieve the dream of a total work of art, where every vocal register is explored, where the breath-taking pre-cinematographic lines of the dialogue are closely linked to an unprecedented flexibility in the orchestral discourse. If Verdi concentrated on the exploration of Shakespearean ambiguity and nihilism, the continually reinterpreted works of the Elizabethan dramatist inspired other movements as well. Maeterlinck found in the blackest of Shakespeare's tragedies, *King Lear* and **Macbeth** *(cat. 70),* the inspiration for his own oneiric theater of hallucinated puppets crushed by a sense of fatality. This suggestive drama inspired authors as different as Ibsen, Strindberg, Wilde and Jarry who shared the aim of a drastic renewal of stage decoration which the Nabi painters would accomplish in an entirely revolutionary manner in the Theater de l'Œuvre from 1890 to 1900.

This tendency towards idealism had been preceded by a realist reaction against the emotive theatricalization of art. Courbet expressed all the powerlessness to act in a poor and lifeless trout. Flaubert, more than any other artist, contributed to violently shattering the middle class sentimentality which poisoned the art of the Salons as it had done that of the stage. In *Madame Bovary* (1856), what could have been a great love scene between Emma and Rodolphe is only a cheap flirtation, interspersed with fragments of speech that are straight out of an agricultural fair. During the performance of *Lucia di Lammermoor,* Emma ventures comparisons between her desires and the action unfolding before her eyes." Lucia, with a brave face, struck up her cavatine in G major ; she complained of love, and asked for wings. In the same way Emma, fleeing life, would have liked to fly into an embrace (...). The voice of the singer seemeds to be the resonance of her own consciousness, the illusion that charmed her, an echo of her own life. But no mortal had ever loved her with such love. "

Even more pitiful is the last encounter between Frederic and Madame Arnoux in *A Sentimental Education* (1869), a fanciful scene for the happy ending of an opera which Flaubert conveys as a distressing void. " She sat down again looking at the clock, while he continued to walk to and fro smoking. Neither of them could find anything more to say. There comes a moment of separation when the person you love is no longer with you. " It would be difficult to push further the use of an objectivity which imposes itself on the consciousness, and rejects all attempts at conventional and reassuring pathos.

The painting of **Degas** is situated exactly in this vein. A lover of opera, and yet an impartial observer of the numerous spectacles that it offers, he consecrated many of his compositions to both ballet and lyric drama. Even a historical work like *Semiramis, Building the Hanging Gardens of Babylon* (1861) only slightly scenographic, was inspired by a performance of Rossini's " Opera seria ". *Mademoiselle Fiocre in the Ballet " The Source "* (fig. 79), is both a portrait of the dancer in costume and the representation of a meditative moment during the ballet. In **The Orchestra of the Opera** (1868, *cat. 66*), shown here, the angle of vision is radically new and the centering gradually shifts towards the musicians, permitting Degas to create a work that is half way between a portrait and a " tableau de genre ". Using the orchestra as a pretext, he assembles his friends, music enthusiasts like Souquet and Pillot around Désiré Dihau, a bassoonist at the Opera who occupies the center of the composition. Several musicians at the Opera are placed exactly in their positions, such as the double-bass player Gouffé, seen from the back, or Altès the flutist, seated behind Dihau. On the far left the composer Chabrier appears in his box. All are turned towards the invisible conductor. On the stage only the legs and the torsos of the dancing ballerinas are distinguishable, illuminated by the footlights. Unlike in the Wagnerian illusion

Fig. 79
Degas: Mademoiselle Fiocre in the ballet
La Source (1866-68)

Fig. 80
Daumier: The Orchestra during the Tragedy (1852)

Fig. 81
Degas: The ballet of *Robert-le-Diable* (1872)

Fig. 82
Degas: Les figurants (the chorists) (1877)

which demands the concealment of the orchestra, Degas topples the traditional representation of the performance by focusing attention on the orchestra pit, then annexing the stage to the pictorial space he has formed.

From this painting onwards, Degas no longer represented performance by coinciding the proscenium arch of the stage with the edges of the composition, or by privileging the focal point of the hall's center, the " mira principis " (or prince's view). Instead, he endeavors to dismantle the theatrical mechanism of illusion by multiplying the slanting views which reveal the painted canvas flats mounted successively on the stage, and expose the agitation in the theater's wings, as in the marvellous monochromatic *Ballet, Rehearsal on Stage* (1874), or the pastel *Les Figurants* (1877, *fig. 82*), which aligns the singers in disordered poses, violently illuminated by the footlights below. Degas arranges nothing, not even fixing the postures, and he never embellishes. Setting out from a position of established reality, he advances to the heart of the representation as if his aesthetic experiences had attained a particular determined density while he animates the spectacle of the performance.

Whether he is occupied with passers by in the street or, figures seen at the races, Degas' intention is always to interrogate movement. It is no longer a question, at least for a painting that aims for life, of striving to attain movement's hypothetical essence. It is in fact, an expression of the moment that is embodied in the actual movement that Muybridge in 1878, unknowingly confirming Degas's research, succeeded in breaking down a horse's gallop.

From now on, developments were rapid. The yearning for a new type of visual entertainment, more mobile and spatially complete, had been susceptible throughout the century, ranging from the heavy " dioramatic " reconstructions of romanticism to Wagnerian lyric opera. It was actually the scientific analysis of photography, literally the " writing of movement ", which was to engender cinema. Starting with Muybridge's discoveries, followed by the chronographic photography of J.E. Marey, and Edison's kinetoscope whereby a film could be

Fig. 83
Muybridge: Horse in movement (1878)

Cat. 80
Lumière: Arrival of a Train at Ciotat

Cat. 80
Lumière: Arrival of a Train at Ciotat

Cat. 81
Le Bargy: The Assassination of the Duke of Guise

Cat. 76
Mucha: La Dame aux Camélias

viewed by one spectator at a time, less than twenty years passed before the brothers **Auguste and Louis Lumière** confronted the public with their invention of "animated photography". During the Christmas holidays of 1895, films of about one minute long were projected at the Grand Café on the Boulevard des Capucines. After **Workers leaving the Lumière factories** the first absolute film in history, nearly 50 films were to follow in 1896, among which is the celebrated **Arrival of a train at La Ciotat Station** *(cat. 80),* where a growing dot is noticable from the beginning, in the background of the landscape, abruptly becoming a menacing locomotive that threatens to attack the audience as if bursting right through the screen.

Louis Lumière appears to have discovered all the expressive possibilities of the moving image, from the first utterings of this new language, in much the same way that Fritz Lang was to explore the faculties of the use of sound in his first talking film " *M* ".

It is surprising to observe to what an extent a recent invention is capable of absorbing modern modes of expression to then become progressively normalized by the effect of an imitative sedimentation. The actor **Le Bargy's « Assassination of the Duke of Guise »** (1908, *cat. 81*) is an excellent illustration of this phenomenon. It was presented as an attempt to ennoble what was still considered as side-show entertainment by filtering it through theatrical tradition (and using the worst possible, that of " The Comédie-Française "). In contrast with the delirious agitation and oneiric inspiration of Meliès, Le Bargy imposed slow, measured and expressive gestures on his troupe, which today have an undeniable disturbing charm : it is sufficient to add that the scenario was by Lavedan and the music by Saint-Saëns, in order to appreciate to what degree a moribund art form could impose its asthmatic breathing upon a language in progress.

Paintings

Brown Ford Madox (1821-1893), English

64 *The finding of Don Juan by Haydee* 1869/1878
(Haïdé découvre le corps de Don Juan)
Oil on canvas (116 × 145 cm)
Signed with monogram and dated bottom left: *FMB -78*
Bequest of Mlle Mathilde Blind, 1897
RF 1133

Chassériau Théodore (1819-1856), French

65 *Romeo and Juliet,* c. 1850
Oil on canvas (50 × 61 cm)
Bequest of the Baron Arthur Chassériau, 1936
RF 3929

Degas Edgar (1834-1917), French

66 *The Orchestra of the Opera,* 1868
(L'Orchestre de l'Opéra)
Oil on canvas (56 × 46 cm)
Signed bottom right: *Degas*
Lent by Mlle Marie Dihau, sister of Désiré Dihau (seen in foreground) from 1923, entered the Louvre in 1935
RF 2417

Delaunay Elie (1828-1891), French

67 *The Plague in Rome,* 1869
(La Peste à Rome)
Oil on canvas (131 × 176.5 cm)
Signed and dated bottom left: *1869 Elie Delaunay*
Acquired at the 1869 Salon
RF 80

Laurens Jean-Paul (1838-1921), French

68 *The Excommunication of Robert the Pious,* 1875
L'excommunication de Robert-le-Pieux)
Oil on canvas (130 × 218 cm)
Signed and dated bottom right: *Jn Paul Laurens, 1875*
Acquired at the 1875 Salon
RF 151

Sketches

Crépinet Alphonse-Nicolas (1826-1892), French

69 *Project for the New Opera House* (Perspective view), 1861
Blacklead and watercolor (50.6 × 68.9 cm)
Signed and dated bottom right: *A. Crépinet architect/Paris, 1861*
Inscription upper right: *Raised in the Seraglio, I know all its detours* (RACINE, BAJAZET)
Acquired in 1983
ARO 1983-1

Merson Luc-Olivier (1846-1920), French

70 *Lady Macbeth Sleep-walking,* circa 1880-1890
(Lady Macbeth somnambule)
Distemper painting on heavy brown paper
(39.3 × 27.9 cm)
Gift of the Friends of the Orsay Museum Society, 1980
RF 38681

Sculpture

Carpeaux Jean-Baptiste (1827-1875), French

71 *Bust of Charles Garnier,* 1869
Bronze (67.6 × 54.5 × 33.6 cm)
Signed: *JB Carpeaux, 1869*
Bequest of Mrs Garnier, 1921
RF 1760

Mercié Antonin (1845-1916), French

72 *David,* 1872
Bronze (184.8 × 76 × 83.2 cm)
Acquired at the 1872 Salon
RF 186

Photographs

Cameron Julia Margaret (1815-1879), English

73 Idylls of the Kings, 1875:
a) *The Beguiling of Merlin*
b) *The Parting of Lancelot and Guenevere*
c) *The Passing of Arthur*
d) *Like a Shatter'd Column Lay the King*
e) *The Princess*
Albumen print from glass negatives (44 × 35 cm
Acquired in 1980
RF 1980-5, -10, -13, -18, -25

Vallou de Villeneuve Julien (1795-1866), French

74 *Portrait of the Actress Rachel* circa 1853
(Portrait de la comédienne Rachel)
Salt print from paper negative (16 × 12 cm)
Gift of the Kodak-Pathé Foundation, 1983
PHO 1983-165 (325)

Posters

Mucha Alphonse (1860-1939), Czechoslovakian

75 *Lorenzaccio,* 1897
(208 × 77 cm)

76 *La Dame aux Camélias,* 1896
(207 × 76.5 cm)
Paris, Musée de la Publicité

Decor Models

Anonymous (from Rubé and Chaperon)

77 *Model for last act of "The Jewess"* by Halévy
(60 × 82 × 65 cm)

78 *Model for "The Prophet"* by Meyerbeer
(60 × 82 × 65 cm)
Paris, Opera Library

Frémiet Emmanuel (1824-1910), French

79 Aquarelles (of the Costumes) for *Joan of Arc* by Mermet,
1876
a) The King (35 × 25.5 cm)
b) Joan (36 × 25)
c) Studies (39 × 25.5)
Paris Opera Library

Films

Lumière Auguste (1862-1954) and Louis (1864-1948),
French

80 Presentation without interruption
December 28th, 1895 showing at the Grand Café, Paris:
Arrival of a Train at Ciotat
Demolition of a Wall
Workers Leaving the Lumière Factory
Baby's Lunch
The Sprinkler Sprinkled
Duration : each film, from 40 seconds to 3 minutes
Paris, Cinémathèque Française

Le Bargy Charles (1858-1936), French

81 *The Assassination of the Duke of Guise* (1908)
(L'Assassinat du Duc de Guise)
Production: Les Films d'Art
Paris, Collection Pathé

Art in the Industrial Environment

The Age of Enlightenment raised the concept of progress to the level of a supreme ideal. In the nineteenth century it was made a verifiable and quantifiable reality, a springboard for the prevalent ideologies. The technological advances applied to the economy were accompanied by social upheavals unknown in Europe up to then : improvements made in agricultural productivity liberated the farm-hand from the rural areas encouraging him to crowd the cities in search of work and to form a proletariat that industry could exploit.

Since the *Communist Manifesto* (1848), Karl Marx had been denouncing the unprecedented servitude produced by capitalism, by which in his opinion it was unconsciously sowing the seeds of its own destruction. Workers organized themselves into unions and political parties while the hope of a socialist utopia as proclaimed by Robert Owen ebbed away, as did the phalansterian vision of Charles Fourier.

Before the advance of " scientific " socialism with its predictions of the State's fatal overthrow, governments took measures to ward off the immediate dangers by giving themselves the means to intervene within the liberal system.

In this manner, Paris rid itself of its insalubrious neighborhoods, long the cauldron of revolutions, under the direction of its Prefect, Baron Haussmann, offering a striking example of the government's new role as social regulator, at the cost of a reactionary denaturalization of the humanistic messages of Saint-Simon or Fourier. State intervention, relatively moderate and diversified compared with other nations, resulted in the gradual establishment of health legislation and a timid control of working conditions.

An altered economic system came into being along with a new kind of political opposition. Corresponding with the emergence of the monopolistic capitalism favored by the more socially concerned governments, the " International Worker " found reinforcement and spread across Europe. From 1848 the

Fig. 84
Lights from the Top of the Tour Eiffel
(1889 World's Fair)

Fig. 85
G. Doré : London Slums (1870)

Cat. 87
Lebas: Petite Roquette Prison (1831)

term "worker" replaced that of "citizen" in the revolutionary vocabulary, revealing a new imagery of protest.

However, the scattered nature of the different movements favored a certain convergence between social-democratic reformers and "socialized" states, as was taking place under Bismarck's Reich. In fact the vertiginous pauperization predicted by Marx and Engels did not take place, and a reformer like Berstein could point to a slow rise in the average standard of living. In the center of this developing society, an enlarged middle-class necessitated a transformation of the authoritative concept as well as social demands. In this perspective, Art, accessible to all, played an important unifying role.

These formative years of history, during which the illiteracy rate dropped due to certain improvements in mass-education and the popularization of knowledge, also witnessed a stabilization of the technological environment. Metallurgy crowded out textiles at the head of industrial production, organic chemistry created essential raw materials, electricity and oil began to be used as energy sources, automobiles appeared and Taylorism began to regulate the rhythm and standards of production.

If a large part of the artistic milieu (the Symbolists in particular) tended to turn their backs on the industrial culture and the middle class mediocrity that it consoled, there were other sectors of society who welcomed these economic and technological mutations with enthusiasm. In its representation of the working

Fig. 86
H. Daumier: The Laundress (1863)

Fig. 87
J.-F. Millet: The Lumberman (1855)

Fig. 88
Ford Madox Brown: Work (1852-65)

classes and their industrial surroundings, in the introduction of iron to architectural styles, in the mass-production of art objects, or in the advent of " design ", Art in the second half of the nineteenth century was violently lashed by the wave of modernization. It is the most revealing manifestation of a changing culture.

"Laborious Classes, Dangerous Classes"

Ever since the seventeenth century there had been a tradition of portraying the lower classes. The Caravaggesques, Le Nain, Velasquez, among others, had often shown the moral and material distress of the poor in a crude fashion. Poverty was rarely shown in isolation, but more often intervening as an allegorical fragment or as a realistic embellishment. In the eighteenth century, picturesque painting became more pronounced: painters like Lepicié or Gainsborough almost automatically associated poverty with youth and innocence, setting it in a relatively turbid atmosphere.

With the Industrial Revolution, depiction of the workers necessarily harbored a new ideological current, especially as the French Revolution had tried to establish a legal system of so-called equality among citizens at a time when class differences were especially flagrant. For a politically committed painter like Daumier, the common man was a rather vague concept which embraced both the proletariat and the lower middle-classes. It is true that at this time typographers, an instructed aristocracy of the working class, often spear-headed social disturbance.

While the worker's movement was organizing itself into co-operatives and unions, painting was falling into step with the naturalist novel. Before Zola, George Sand, Eugène Sue, and Victor Hugo had agitated the conscience of society under both the July Monarchy and the Second Empire. However, they never quite reached the visionary power of Dickens, who depicted the stark panorama of the London industrial jungle.

French social structure remained mostly agrarian until the end of the century. This was accentuated by the return to protectionism after the crisis of 1873. In 1851, France still counted 75 % of its population in its rural areas ; on the eve of the First World War, over 50 % dwelt in the country-side compared to only 25 % in England. Jean-François Millet (1814-1875) painted a series of idealized rural scenes during the 1850's in such paintings as *The Planter* (1850) and *The Gleeners* (1857) while Jules Breton (1827-1906), Alphonse Legros (1837-1899) and Wilhelm Leibl (1844-1900) in Germany emphasized a kind of ethnographical primitivism. Their aim was to record the disappearing rural life styles and to confer an uncorruptible nobility upon the work ethic. The 1848 Revolution had recognized labor as a civil right and elevated it to a position of timeless value, almost of heroic allegory, that was given expression in the monumental painting entitled *Work* by Ford Madox Brown. (1857-65)

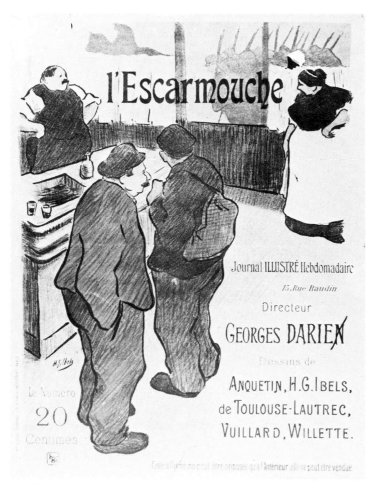

Cat. 86
Ibels: L'Escarmouche

With Courbet the fusion between realism and social testimony was accomplished. His *Stone-breakers* (1849) had no further allegorical significance beyond their simple physical presence. For Courbet it was a question of depicting what really existed; he refused to idealize, rejecting the sentimental anecdote, the small format and the stable hierarchies on the canvas. Yet his representations of workers, actually rather infrequent, did not shock his contemporaries more than his *Bathers, The Burial at Ornans* or *The Ladies of the Village,* where it was the bourgeoisie whom he depicted. Realism itself was unacceptable to the general public because it transformed the conventional principles governing the working class, just as the workers themselves were slowly becoming conscious of their alienation and consequently getting organized.

Cat. 85
Chéret: *La Terre* by Zola

From now on for over half a century, the destiny of "socially committed" painting was closely bound to realism. Its course was somewhat parallel to that of the naturalist novel, whose principal inspiration came from Emile Zola, an admirer of both Taine and Darwin. In his novels *L'Assommoir* (1877) and *Germinal* (1885) he engaged in social inquiries that evoke the merciless observation of a physician's clinical lucidity.

During the opening years of the Third Republic, the Paris Salon opened its doors to sculpture and painting that represented the proletariat at work. Even though Jules Breton remained loyal to the quasi-biblical transfiguration of the rustic world (his *Shepherd's Star* dates from 1887), the new realist generation shifted towards paintings of small urban trades in the heart of "Moloch Town" as described in Zola's *Ventre de Paris.* Few works, especially by those who gave in to the public's conception of the urban worker, even though they occasionally possessed a haunting realistic precision, can equal the breadth of vision attained by the great novelist: we should note however, Bastien Lepage's *London Bootblack* (1882), Raffaeli's *Ragman,* Victor Gabriel Gilbert's *A Corner of the Fish Market in the Morning* (1880), and Gervex's *Heavy Porters* (1881). Only the Belgian realist school escaped a folkloric and sentimental depiction of the worker's condition by bestowing an epic quality on works such as *The Ages of the Worker* (1895) by Léon Frédéric or *The Immigrants* (1894) by Xavier Mellery. Meanwhile, credit must be given to the Italian G. Pellizza da Volpedo for having created the only absolute masterpiece of the genre with his *Fourth Estate* (1901, *fig. 89*), in which a group of strikers are portrayed facing the spectator within a panoramic view, surrounded by powdery light.

The peasant world nevertheless retained its illustrators who never wearied of wandering over the furrows marked out by Jean-François Millet. Confronted to industrialization which was digging its claws in everywhere, the peasantry, still extremely numerous at the end of the century, appeared to be evolving rather slowly. Exaggerating a mood already expressed by Balzac in *Les Paysans* (1846), **Zola** in his novel **La Terre** (1887, *cat. 85*) offered a breathtaking expressionistic vision of a hostile, threatening and extremely backward environment.

Jules Bastien-Lepage had expressed similar feelings in **The Haymakers** *(cat. 83)* which made the greatest impression on the critics of all the works

Fig. 89
G. Pellizza da Volpedo: The Fourth Estate
(1898-1901)

Cat. 83
Bastien-Lepage: The Hay Makers

exhibited at the 1878 Salon. It was as though the two protagonists of *L'Angélus* by Millet (1858-1859) were to be found by the spectator hours before the performance of their evening vespers, beaten down into the grass by their fatigue and the midday heat. Paul Mantz enthused, "...it is the unrelenting and loyal reproduction of a young peasant girl who has never looked at herself in the mirror of the ideal [...] her eyes are fixed upon a mysterious horizon ; (she) is absorbed by an overwhelming thought, by a sort of instinctive revery, the intensity of which is heightened by the rapturous smell of freshly cut grass. " Zola covered the young painter, upon whom he placed the hopes of naturalism, with great praise : " His superiority over the Impressionist painters is summed up in this fact ; he knows how to convey his impressions. " The Realists at the end of the century, torn between the shock of discovering the backwardness of country mentality and a resistance to the normalization imposed by the urban culture, extolled the naïve purity of the rural world. Not only Léon L'Hermitte and Julien Dupré, but all of the painters who devoted themselves to rural life fatally confused painting with moralizing illustration.

Unfortunately, good intentions do not necessarily lead to good painting, as is proved by the work of the " Réalistes-Pompiers " (traditionalist) painters at the end of the century. Pascal Dagnan-Bouveret (1852-1929), Henri Geoffroy (1853-1924), or Alfred Roll (1847-1919) imagined themselves to have attained the sacred core of the human condition when in fact they were merely embroidering with the saccharine thread of the picturesque. From very different socio-political conditions, they foreshadowed all the failed painters who threw themselves into working-class realism and became the acolytes of Hitlerian and Stalinist aestheticism. As early as the end of the century, there were already a number of ready-made populist formulas.

And what of the Impressionists ? It is currently said (by way of compensation for excessive aesthetic evolution) that the Impressionists were bourgeois figures who turned their backs on the social problems of their time. The ironing women *(fig. 90)* and the street girls of Degas, the rowers in straw-hats by Renoir, the peasants of Pissarro, the suburbs of Seurat and above all the innumerable representations of work by Van Gogh give evidence to the contrary. In fact, it is rather their objective vision, their refusal to moralize which disturbs and is over-rapidly interpreted as indifference or detachment.

Impressionism inherited certain ambiguities from Realism because it protested in a similar way against the cynicism of the new ruling classes and the expression of a bourgeois ideology that placed its trust in the exploration of realism. This ambiguity is nowhere more evident than in *The Floor Scrapers* (1875, *fig. 91*) by G. Caillebotte, if only because of its stylistic characteristics : the plunging perspective, the assymmetry and the void which invades the composition giving this work a quality of audacity similar to that found in the contemporary works of his friend Degas ; the treatment still resembles the academic instruction of his teacher, Bonnat.

Caillebotte, the accomplished bourgeois, observed these workmen planing

Fig. 90
Degas : The Ironers (1884)

Fig. 91
Caillebotte : The Floor-Scrapers (1875)

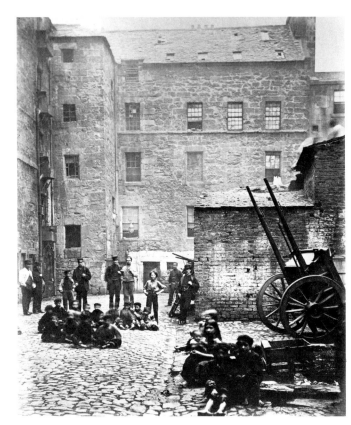

Cat. 92
Annan: Glasgow, Streets and Closes

wood during the renovation of his family's hôtel on the rue de Miromesnil. He brought their work methods and tools (planes, drawing knives, hammers, etc.) to the canvas respectfully and with a quasi-photographic precision, but at no time did he lapse into picturesqueness or social denunciation.

His observation allowed him to reveal the evident plastic beauty of a moment of pure but well organized realism. These three bodies working at the same task gave him the opportunity to break up the kinetic coherence of action into three phases, bathing them in a soft bluish light. Nevertheless certain critics protested against the vulgarity of the subject as they had against his *House Painters*.

If Realist painting, on the fringes of Impressionism was partially bound to social statement, it was only natural that photography continued to play a more central role as an irrefutable proof, a testimony which aroused the emotions of political society.

The report by **Thomas W. Annan: Glasgow, Streets and Closes** (1867, *cat. 92*) commissioned by a special parliamentary committee (not to forget the ensemble of images devoted to on **The Vincennes Imperial Asylum** commissioned from **Charles Nègre** by Napoleon III in 1859, *cat. 94*) constitutes the first sociological inquiry illustrated by photographers. All of the possible degradation and desolation of a nineteenth century industrial city is contained in these documents which insist upon the suffocating atmosphere and the absence of any life, except for a brief mention of the human presence. Despite a rather formal

Cat. 94
Nègre: Workers' Meal at the Vincennes Asylum

Cat. 93
Hine: Italian Immigrants

style of composition, the results are startling. They not only gave rise to other inquiries such as *Street Life in London* (1877) by Adoph Smith, but they also played a major role in determining a more efficient policy of social welfare.

The same effect was produced in the United States where Jacob A. Riis' crushing testimonies published in *How the Other Half Lives* (1890) attracted the attention of political reformers like Theodore Roosevelt.

In a comparable vein, the photographer and sociologist **Lewis W. Hines** published a series of documents concerning the crowding of Second Wave immigrants (Italians, Greeks, Turks, Poles, etc.) into the Ellis Island facilities. The very sophisticated composition of his **Italian Immigrants** (1905, *cat. 93*) evokes the majestic balance of certain paintings on the *Madonna and Child* theme by Correggio or by Andrea del Sarto, far removed from other photographs, which show a much cruder violence. This outburst of pictorialism brings to mind some of the bitter beauty of the first accounts of immigration in F.M. Brown's *The Last of England* (1852-1855). Later on, the talent of Hine would serve in a crusade against child labor in coal mines and textile mills.

The Industrial Inferno

Industrial sites were not frequent in painting before our own century: they seemed to be a subject lacking in poetry. And yet their formal characteristics were already fixed by artists before the end of the eighteenth century, with a predilection for nocturnal settings where violent contrasts of light surrounded the activity of blast furnaces, as in the famous views of Coalbrookdale by Philip de Loutherbourg (1740-1812).

When industrial power has attracted the homeless peasant from the countryside to the tentacular metropolis, then images of hell fire will be superimposed upon the legions of mechanical ghost-puppets working in the ever-grey Gehena. As Linda Nochlin stated, everything that belongs to the forges, swamps, mines or factories is associated with an infernal visual vocabulary. From Blake to Dickens, from John Martin to Gustave Doré *(fig. 85),* the illustrator of London, the denunciation of the incredible misery upon which capitalism was built is increased by a strong mistrust of the uncontrollable technological progress, through which Evil pursues its destructive work.

With **The Blast Furnace** (1893) by **Fernand Cormon** *(cat. 82)* the ideological jump was flagrant; progress and industrialization were seen as positive values. The blast furnace became a site permitting an exaltation of work heroism while at the same time offering easy chiaroscuro effects such as those of François Bonhommé in a series of paintings devoted to factories in Le Creusot during the Second Empire.

On the other hand, a certain restlessness seems to filter through the more somber visions of the Belgian Constantin Meunier's *The Casting in Ongrée* and *The Black Country* which approach the feeling of the poet Emile Verhaeren, for whom the factories were:

> "Granite rectangles and brick monuments,
> Long black walls stretching for leagues
> Immense, amidst the suburbs."

The American **Lionel Walden** was, for his part, sensitive to the strange fascination offered by the **Docks of Cardiff** (1896, *cat. 84*) which appear to be animated by a life of their own. This monochromatic desert, asceptic and criss-crossed by rails, foreshadows the future geometrical and industrial visions of Charles Sheeler and Ralston Crawford.

The industrial landscape had its own mysterious logic. From its cold and obsessional regularity, there emerged an indistinct and magical anxiety. The metaphysical terror facing the flamboyant disorder produced by uncontrollable capitalism slowly metamorphized into a subtle feeling of both attraction and repulsion towards sites where the absurd was materializing.

Fig. 92
Monet: St-Lazare Station (1877)

Fig. 93
Seurat: Suburbs (1883)

Cat. 82
Cormon: The Blast Furnace

Cat. 84
Walden: The Docks of Cardiff

Iron Architecture

The painter Lantier in Zola's *L'Œuvre* prophesied that "iron will kill the stone". Moreover, the author himself signed a petition of artists opposed to the construction of the Eiffel Tower that "even commercial America wouldn't want."

Iron architecture was then a limitless source of controversy and ambiguous judgement, whereas today the interlacing of metallic structures has become the best visual short-cut of the twentieth century. Baltard consented almost with reluctance to the construction of the iron umbrellas that the Prefect Haussmann had requested for the new Halles of Paris, and the new visible metallic structure of Labrouste's *Imperial Library (fig. 94)* was for many an eyesore. Eclectism was ready to accept a metal framework only if it were concealed by the traditional coating. A mere handful of architects understood that the assertion of a new technique demanded a radical reform of architectural language which was to comply more and more with functional necessity.

The only iron structured buildings accepted without too much controversy were the World's Fair Pavilions, in which international products, confronting each other, were exhibited throughout the second half of the century owing to a momentary relaxation of trade restrictions.

The first World's Fair held in London in 1851 took place in the giant nave of the Crystal Palace which now appears as a perfect and unsurpassed model of its type. Sir Joseph Paxton (1803-1865), its creator, was not an architect, but in fact a builder of green-houses. Refusing traditional wall construction, he erected one of the lightest and most transparent edifices of all time. Despite its colossal dimensions (600 meters long), he resolved all of the inherent problems of metallic construction : water run-off (with cast iron mountings), condensation of humidity, ventilation, and so on. Few contemporaries understood that a new phase of architecture had begun, mainly because this building had been conceived as a pavilion, an ephemeral and ready-to-dismantle construction, which would not dare rival other "real" monuments.

Iron architecture would prove to be even more audacious at later World's Fairs, events which amidst the illusionary "harmony of nations" paraded the dominant tastes of the bourgeoisie and the munificence of "good governments" before the eyes of a public overwhelmed by so much ostentation.

If the 1855 Paris Fair returned to a heavy wall construction covered by a glass cupola, the 1867 Fair proposed a more "temporary" look with its concentric ovals imprisonning a garden. Each nation had a designated section leading the official program to exclaim that "a walk around this circular palace is like embarking on a world tour."

These appeasing words perfectly crystalized the ideal of concord which presided in the organization of a World's Fair ; it is nevertheless necessary to keep in mind the high commercial stakes and ruthless competition which were also its underlying conditions.

Fig. 94
Labrouste: Imperial Library, Paris (1855-1868)

Fig. 95
Hall of Machines (1889 World's Fair)

Until the 1889 Paris World's Fair, no new buildings marked any important step in metallic construction. A new direction was given by the immense *Hall of Machines* by Dutert and Contamin *(figs 95 and 96),* set up around one main arc with no intermediary support, and intersected by numerous mobile viewing platforms. This advance was confirmed by the construction of the **Eiffel Tower** (the different stages of its construction are shown here through a number of **photographs** by unknown artists, *cats. 95 and 88*). The unprecedented dimensions of these structures succeeded in altering the role of this architecture and generated a whole new way of considering a monument : iron could at last take on a symbolic meaning without alluding to earlier architecture. A mere technological achievement at first, the Eiffel Tower became a historical phenomenon — by its formal development it redefined the entire surrounding urban space, a space which painters of modernism from Seurat to Delaunay would translate into poetry.

Cat. 88
Toussaint : Project for the Eiffel Tower

Fig. 96
Hall of Machines (1889 World's Fair)
The mobile platforms

Cat. 95
Anonymous: Eiffel Tower in construction

Cat. 95
Anonymous: Eiffel Tower in construction

The Multiplied Object

A consequence of the accumulation of capital and the emergence of a middle-class with its own conception of what was beautiful and desirable was the mass-production of the object, another chief characteristic of the Industrial Revolution. The role of initiator undoubtedly belonged to photography which brought to an end the inherent uniqueness of the art object, until then to be found only in the hands of a few. It was the first activity which combined science and art, thus inaugurating the uncontested reign of the image over discourse and " preparing our species for this infirmity so that we would no longer be capable of imagining duration effectively or symbolically. " (Roland Barthes).

The social changes were a factor that permitted this phenomenon : economic growth, bound to industrial development, released an inexhaustible wealth which accumulated in the hands of entrepreneurs, directors and financiers all of whom tried to assimilate the aesthetic principles of the former ruling class, but for whom abundance remained fatally synonymous with refined taste. For a liberal economic system where the following day could bring ruin, abundance and accumulation were reassuring, as the exterior signs of success, of the victory over poverty. Ludwig Feuerbach, the German philosopher, expressed his grief : " Our era prefers the image to the original, representation to reality, appearence to being. "

An original work of art copied out infitely in any and every material ends up being considered on the same level as its replicas. The image and the surface prevail over the essence of the work and the debasing of the material becomes the inevitable corollary of profusion. Therefore it was unsurprising that no stylistic idiom dominated the scene. Victorian eclecticism, also found with slight variations in Germany, France and the United States embraced all styles from modified classicism to Neo-Gothic, from the Renaissance to Neo-Rococo. A style such as the newly developed Neo-Classicism was used repeatedly on request and survived throughout the nineteenth century as a possible last resort, independant of the profound evolution affecting form.

Objects for everyday use underwent new transformations, for example : bedside lamps were produced in the form of ionic columns with fancy gabled lampshades ; rococo-gothic writing desks could be transformed into beds. To the inevitable observer the applied arts catalogue of the Crystal Palace Fair demonstrated the pitiful state of Western decorative arts, offering a large number of what in a later age would have been taken for surrealist collages ; works that Max Ernst himself would not have needed to corrupt.

The mid-nineteenth century saw the priviledged expression of a triumphant eclecticism, a precise moment in the evolution of aesthetic sentiment, soon to be swept aside by the inevitable reactions. Art, beleaguered and reduced by mass-production, a state which still exists, was at times amplified by feverish outbursts of Kitsch.

From sheet metal statues to chromolithographs and post cards, aesthetic

Cat. 96
Carpeaux: The Imperial Prince and His Dog Nero

pleasure exploded into a multitude of small gratifications which were among the most noticeable expressions of a society of mass-consumption. This "art of happiness", an irreducible characteristic of modern life, opened a new chapter in the history of taste. It was the counterpart of standardization and uniformity imposed by a monopolistic capitalism, a supply of sentimentality secreted by the Machine Age, as if to exonerate itself.

The **Imperial Prince and His Dog Nero** *(cat. 96)* by **J.B. Carpeaux** (1865), illustrates this point in various ways. To begin with, it was commissioned by Napoleon III for the same purposes as any political image, that is to be used for

Cat. 97
Carpeaux: Child and Dog

soliciting allegiance to the monarchy. By sculpting the heir to the throne in a comfortable and relaxed pose, Carpeaux suggested the dynasty's continuity while avoiding the arrogance typical of official portraits. A reproduction in silver plated bronze of the marble original was placed in the Paris Hotel de Ville and further replicas were likewise bought by the other city halls to be placed next to the Emperor's bust, only to be quickly replaced by as many Mariannes, the French Republic's traditional effigy. The commercial success of the work did not decline with the Empire's fall. Under the neutral title **Child with Dog** *(cat. 97)* the Carpeaux workshops followed by those of Barbedienne and Christophle, reproduced bronze statues of all sizes, and the Sevres Manufacturers even made three different sized sets of biscuit ware.

Nevertheless, the popularity of *Child with Dog* was not as great as another unrivalled success : the **Statue of Liberty** by **Bartholdi** *(cat. 98)*. Without a doubt, this is one of the most frequently reproduced images ever, behind which an entire nation not only recognizes itself, but also finds a conception of democracy that transcends national pride. The iconographic sources of the original are to be found in the colossal statues of the Baroque and Canova, with later modifications representing the revolutionary virtues ; the statue's propagation is the miraculous meeting point of both the democratic ideal and industrial mass production. It is no coincidence that the statue's smelter Gaget, who went to New York for the inauguration with his suitcase full of small replicas should find his name (with a new spelling reflecting its American pronunciation) attached all sorts of small objects without any artistic or utilitary use. The latest link in a long chain evolving from the religious relic, the gadget, at times an object of kitsch, began its long existence of metamorphosis through a reduction designed to rehabilitate the sacred quality of the original object.

Cat. 98
Bartholdi: Statue of Liberty

Design

Behind the origins of the English *Arts and Crafts* movement there existed a profound hostility towards industrial mechanization and the environment it created. Not only was it demeaning the aesthetic, but it was also enslaving man. For John Ruskin and William Morris it was necessary to return to the medieval ideal of harmony and balance in the production process, where a determinant role was given to the know-how and ingenuity of the craftsman.

Ruskin expressed total repulsion towards the idea of industry but he was not adverse to its effects on the taste of his time ; for instance, his appreciation of the hypothetical gothic revival. Morris, devoted to creation, did not harbor the same fears as his friend towards the machine.

After the construction and decoration of his *Red House* at Upton in 1859, Morris surrounded himself with such artists as Burne-Jones, Rossetti, Brown, Ph. Webb and in 1862 founded the firm *Morris and Company (fig. 99)* which produced furniture, glassware, wallpaper etc. In his effort to transform the human environment from architecture down to the tiniest of its decorative objects, Morris, with a coherent creative determination, foreshadowed the great masters of Art Nouveau, Van de Velde and Hoffmann, but found himself in contradiction between a desire to create works '' for the people '' and the very high cost of production which implied a more well-to-do clientele.

Morris' admirable struggle to revive the lost dignity of labor by attempting to effect the structure of society proposed a similar ambiguity of an ideological split between nostalgia for the '' radiant '' Middle Ages and an attraction to scientific socialism. He was thus at the forefront of a double impulse, obliged to justify the search undertaken by numerous intellectuals (the utilitarian school of John Stuart

Fig. 97
Catalogue of the Crystal Palace, 1851

Fig. 98
Catalogue of the Crystal Palace, 1851

Fig. 99
W. Morris : Chintz fabrics (1891)

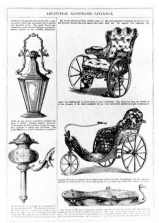

Cat. 91
Viollet-le-Duc: Wallpaper

Mill in particular) for a viable alternative to industry, while at the same time the renewal of craftsmanship was providing him with better models for industry.

Consequently, his stained glass windows, chintz fabrics and wallpaper met with great success. He had been preceeded in this area by **Viollet-le-Duc** *(cats. 89, 90, 91)* for whom architecture encompassed not only masonry but also the final touches. **The wallpaper** that he presents in his **History of a Home** (1873) evokes a number of different styles: "neo-pompeian" geometrics containing floral pre-Japanese motifs with subtle grotesque interlacings. He states, "The large grain of the canvas reproduces the texture of tapestry well, and the distemper takes on the flat tones of wool." Using painting also kept production costs to a minimum. Like Morris, Viollet-le-Duc insisted upon the designer's knowledge of technical procedure, so that he would not propose objects whose production could not be carried out.

England in the 1870's, at the height of its industrial power, was the privileged

laboratory of industrial design: the profusion of inventions meant that new shapes would gradually adapt to their enlarged role. Alexander Graham Bell's first telephone (1876) resembled an old miniature printing press and was later redesigned to resemble the modern telephone when it was planned for home or office use.

The technological environment slid into definite categories, except for the more simplified curves thought up to facilitate work on the assembly line: the bicycle, the electric light bulb, the camera, the typewriter etc. With the new production methods, the role of the industrial designer disassociated itself from that of the engineer and became the essential link between the artistic milieu and the technological environment.

This did not prevent the architect at the dawning of Art Nouveau from asserting his role as a designer particularly as the idea of decoration could only be separated with difficulty from that of the completed structure. In this way the **decorative motifs cast in iron by Hector Guimard** *(cats. 99, 100, 101)* for

Fig. 100
Typewriter (c. 1880)

Cat. 99
Guimard: Central Motif for Stone Balcony

Fig. 101
The evolution of bicycle

Cat. 100
Guimard: Eaves Ornament

Cat. 101
Guimard: Vase and Pedestal

Cat. 105
Van de Velde: Bloemenwerf Chair

Cat. 106
Wright: Chair

Parisian apartment buildings, such as the building in the avenue Mozart or the synagogue in the rue Pavée, offer the same multi-directional floral expansions as the vegetal ironwork that surrounds the Metro entrances. Guimard translated the irrepressible dynamism of the curved line into his urban furnishings and in this way stated Art Nouveau's social discourses. Despite their divergent aesthetics, the intention is comparable to that of Horta in Brussels or Otto Wagner in Vienna. The industrial city's disorder was to be corrected through a coherent vision of aesthetics that would establish a harmony with nature's vital impulses.

This was the case with **Van de Velde** who in his home furnishings attempted to convey this same feeling. His **Bloemenwerf chair** (1897-1899, *cat. 105*) in the solid wood of traditional craftsmanship is tautly designed and refuses any superficial embellishment. Its centrifugal organic development around the elegant curve of its frame, made it a work similar to the metal architecture of the day. The chair was put to use in the editorial room of the symbolist *Revue Blanche*.

Fig. 102
J. Hoffmann: Armchair

Cat. 104
Thonet: Chairs

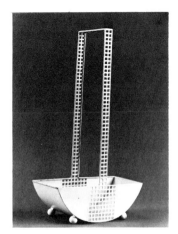

Fig. 103
J. Hoffmann: Basket

The chair *(cat. 106)* by **Frank Lloyd Wright** (1908) constructed for the home of Isabel Roberts goes even further in the austere simplification of a form that is executed by a machine, " the normal tool of civilization. " Largely inspired by Japanese screens, the high back formed by separate wooden laths permits a demarcation of the dining room area while conserving the transparency of the space as a whole — the pieces of furniture are in this way organically incorporated into the architecture of their surroundings.

Using a different approach, the *Wiener Werkstätte* (Viennese Workshop) organized by Joseph Hoffmann and Koloman Moser (from 1903) attained the same type of concision in the structural design of many works. There also existed a *Biedermeier* tradition of independant design in Austria and southern Germany, remarkable for its simplicity of form. The most striking example in a somewhat lighter vein is the inexhaustible range of **arm-chairs and chairs by Michael Thonet** *(cat. 104)*. Made from beechwood which had been molded through heat (the Bentwood process), their functional line has had an uninterrupted success up to our day.

The intentions of both Hoffmann and Moser were entirely in line with the first attempts to harmonize artistic creation with contemporary society. The **cutlery by Hoffmann** *(cat. 102)* was created for the well-known Café Fledermaus (1907), decorated like a sort of black and white jewel box, where the Viennese avant-garde congregated. The pure lines of this set foreshadowed Bauhaus functionalism, showing a concern for refinement with the small monogram that reflects the decorative effect of the entire café.

The fluid animation of **Kolo Moser's glass works** *(cat. 103),* where the austere handle of the decanter is opposed to the gracious curves of the vase's body originate in a comparable aestheticism that is also attached to the Austrian tradition, illustrated in Ludwig Lobmeyr's " Musselinglass " (1856).

In discussing these craftsmen, it is necessary to mention that their products belonged to an art which, despite its very generous principles, had evolved into an art which was now addressing an elite.

Cat. 102
Hoffmann: Cutlery

Cat. 103
Moser: Glass-ware

Painting

Cormon Fernand (1854-1924), French

82 *The Blast Furnace,* 1893
(La Forge)
Oil on canvas (59 × 78 cm)
Signed and dated bottom left: *F. Cormon 93*
Acquired from the Salon of French Artists in 1894
RF 891

Bastien-Lepage Jules (1848-1884), French

83 *The Hay Makers,* 1877
(Les foins)
Oil on canvas (180 × 195 cm)
Signed bottom left: *Damvilliers, Bastien-Lepage*
Acquired in 1885
RF 2718

Walden Lionel (1861-1933), American

84 *The Docks of Cardiff,* 1894
(Docks de Cardiff)
(127 × 193 cm)
Signed and dated bottom right: *Lionel Walden 1894*
Acquired from the Salon of French Artists in 1896
RF 1052

Poster

Chéret Jules (1836-1932), French

85 "La Terre" by Zola
Poster (222 × 81 cm)
Paris, *Musée de la Publicité*

Ibels Gabriel (1867-1936), French

86 *L'Escarmouche,* (The skirmish), 1893
Poster (65 × 50.5 cm)
Paris, *Musée de la Publicité*

Architectural Design

Lebas Hippolyte (1782-1867), French

87 *Petite Roquette Prison (1831)*
Aquarelle (35 × 47.8 cm)
Signed bottom right: *h. Lebas*
Acquired in 1980
ARO 1980-90

Toussaint Henri (1849-1911), French

88 *Project for the Eiffel Tower (c. 1900)*
(Projet d'habillage de la tour Eiffel) (90 × 114.5 cm)
Gift of Mrs Solange Granet, of Mrs Bernard Granet and her children, 1981
ARO 1981-931

Viollet-le-Duc Eugène-Emmanuel (1814-1879), French

Three Projects of wall-canvas for "History of a House"
1870-1873

89 Aquarelle (19.2 × 11.2 cm)

90 Aquarelle (19.4 × 11.5 cm)

91 Aquarelle «19.6 × 11.2 cm)
All signed bottom right: *EVle D*
Acquired in 1980
ARO 1980-95, -96, -97

Photography

Annan Thomas (1829-1887), English

92 *Glasgow, Streets and Closes,* 1867
Albumen print from collodion glass negative
(30.2 × 38 cm)
a/ *Saltmarket*
b/ *High Street*
Acquired in London, 1983
PHO 1983-50 and 62

Hine Lewis W. (1874-1920), American

93 *Italian Immigrants,* 1905
Silver print
(22.5 × 18.7 cm)
Acquired in 1984
PHO 1984-58

Nègre Charles (1820-1880), French

94 *Workers Meal at the Vincennes Imperial Asylum,* 1859
Albumen silver print from collodion glass negative
(34.2 × 42.5 cm)
Gift from the Kodak-Pathé Foundation, Paris 1983
PHO 1983-165 (210)

Anonymous

95 *Photographs of the Eiffel Tower construction,* 1889
(13 × 8.5 cm)
Acquired in 1984
PHO 1985-125

Sculpture

Carpeaux Jean-Baptiste (1827-1875), French

96 *The Imperial Prince and His Dog Nero,* 1865
Bronze (68.3 × 32.5 × 30.2 cm)
Signed: JB CARPEAUX AUX TUILERIES, 1865
RF 651

97 *Child and Dog*
Biscuit-ware (40.5 cm)
Sèvres Museum
Inv. 17449

98 **Bartholdi** Frédéric-Auguste
Liberty (1889)
Bronze (287 × 105 × 75 cm)
Signed: A. BARTHOLDI, 15 / DE / NOVEMBRE / 1889
Acquired by the Musée du Luxembourg, 1901
French Senate

Objets d'art

Guimard Hector (1867-1942), French

99 *Central Motif for Stone Balcony,* 1905-1907
Works in cast-iron by the St. Dizier Foundry
(35 × 93.5 cm)
Donated by Mme de Menil, 1981
OAO 636

100 *Eaves Ornament,* 1905-1907
Works in cast-iron by the St. Dizier Foundry
(32 × 70 cm)
Donated by Mme de Menil in 1981
OAO 612

101 *Vase and pedestal,* 1905-1907
(135.5 × 59 × 45 cm)
Donated by Mme Menil, 1981
OAO 622 (1-2)

Hoffmann Joseph (1870-1956), Austrian

102 *Cutlery,* 1907
(Ménagère) (11 items)
Made at the Wiener Werkstätte
Silver-Plated
Acquired in 1981
OAO 57 (1-11)

Moser Koloman (1868-1918), Austrian

103 *Glass-ware,* c. 1899
Fabricated by A. Bakalowits and Sons in Vienna
Acquired in 1981
OAO 545 (1-2), 546 (2), 547 (2), 548 (1-2), 549 (1)
Thonet Brothers (Franz, Michael, August, Josef, Jacob);
Austrian Firm created in 1853, Vienna

104 *3 Chairs* (Cat. Thonet 1888, n. 4, 21, 51)
Bentwood (93 × 43 × 51 cm)
Acquired in 1984

Van de Velde Henry (1863-1957), Belgian

105 *Chair,* 1897-99
Oak and Leather
(96 × 47 × 50.8 cm)
Acquired in 1981
OAO 525

Wright Frank Lloyd (1867-1959), American

106 *Chair,* 1908
Oak and Leather (125 × 45 × 51 cm)
Acquired in 1982
OAO 866

Japonisme

Fig. 104
Hokusai: The Wave

Fig. 105
Hiroshige: The Way to Tokaido

Fig. 106
Whistler: Old Battersea Bridge (1872-5)

" ...With our experience the world has contracted,
And the equator is now but an extremely narrow ring. "

The end of the nineteenth century only served as a confirmation of these lines from Vigny. Once the tide of Orientalism had been exhausted, it was necessary to turn the limits of the cultural horizon towards other unknown shores. And if industrialized Europe was not yet ready to take an interest in " primitive " art, and the Tropics still seemed somewhat dismal, the Empire of the Rising Sun on the opposite side of the globe, displayed the magical reflections of a world turned upside down. It was exactly the refined Cipangu that Christopher Columbus had sought, at the same time very distant due to its medieval tradition and yet close at hand because of an amazing ability to adapt.

The European way of looking at the Japanese experience demanded a new category of openmindedness towards the world. The image that this remote empire offered could not simply be stated in a few easy clichés. Encyclopedists had already expressed their admiration for its remarkable population, the only one in Asia that had never been conquered and that protected its culture by closing itself off entirely from the outside world. Japan thus benefited from immense prestige at the moment when the United States, followed by the European powers, compelled it to open up its frontiers.

From this country came the art of the print, corresponding with research being undertaken by western avant-garde artists, along with art objects of such refinement that beside them the neighboring western production proudly exhibited at the first World's Fairs seemed to pale. More surprising still was the rapidity with which the country would industrialize, modernizing its society and its army, soon to become the most powerful in the Far East. At the end of the nineteenth century, Japan participated in the *Break-up of China,* and definitively entered the club of world powers, when in 1905, she wrestled the Russian Empire to the ground ; and this, by remaining totally attached to the secular tradition that so commanded the admiration of Europeans : respect for the Emperor as divine personage, the cult of ancestors, ardent patriotism, and so on.

Japan was the first obstacle which arose in the colonial normalization process undertaken by the world powers.

Japanese objets d'art were first exhibited at the London 1862 World's Fair. From that moment on, such enraptured enthusiasts as Arthur Liberty and Edward Godwin, became its propagators. The collecting of prints had already existed for a number of years ; these famous *ukiyo-e* prints were considered by the Japanese as a minor genre compared with the paintings jealously enclosed in their shrines.

Among the first Japonists in Paris were the Goncourt brothers, Philip Burty, Théophile Gautier and Baudelaire, all regular visitors at " The Chinese Gate ", the gallery of Japanese art and handicrafts which opened in 1860, on the rue de Rivoli, near the Louvre. Soon, the shop was frequented by Tissot, Manet, Degas, Carolus-Duran, Zola (of whom Manet painted a portrait in 1868 in front of a print by Kuniaki II and a folding-screen, *fig. 4*), and of course Whistler, the first to integrate the extremely particular Japanese perspective into his own style. With few exceptions, the Japanese wave would influence only the artistic avant-garde at the end of the Second Empire.

During the Paris 1867 World's Fair, the large French public and the crowds of foreign visitors were able to discover the art of Japan. The extremely refined laquer-ware and porcelaine techniques were highly admired. Soon the industrialist Cernuschi toured Japan with the critic Théodore Duret, and then exhibited his collection of art objects at the " Palais de l'Industrie " in 1873. In the same year the noted linguist Léon de Rosny organized the first Orientalist convention dedicated to Japan. Due to the growing demand, Siegfried Bing went to Japan in 1875 for his supplies and opened a boutique in 1877.

It was therefore with a considerably strengthened public image that Japan participated in the Paris World's Fair of 1878, where the Japanese model " farm " was a great success *(fig. 107, 108)*. In a well-known article in the *Fine Arts Gazette*, " Japan in Paris ", the critic Ernest Chesneau summarized the impact made by the Japanese phenomenon over the previous twenty years : " The painters did not even try to resist. With their intelligence they knew how to direct the action that was to influence their own talent. Each one assimilated from Japanese art the qualities which had the greatest affinities with their own gifts (...) all found a confirmation of, rather than an inspiration for, their personal methods of seeing, feeling, understanding and interpreting nature. From this emerged an increase in originality instead of a timid submission to Japanese Art. "

For most artists, Japan was only an additional source of eclecticism ; for the avant-garde it became the justification for numerous innovations : surprising framing of subjects, aerial perspectives, asymmetrical compositions, the observation of nature, a subtler sense of color, and an unrestrained dialectic between skill and fortuity.

Fig. 107
1878 World's Fair, Paris ; The Japanese Farm

Fig. 108
1878 World's Fair, Paris ; The Japanese Farm

Fig. 109
Torii Kiyonaga : The Sixth Month,
from *Twelve Month in the South* (1784)

Fig. 110
Whistler : The Balcony (1864-1870)

Whereas Japan pressed on with the Westernization program, Art Nouveau in its early stages asserted itself by the use of the main principles of Japanese decoration. In 1888, Siegfried Bing published the magazine *Le Japon Artistique.* This was the year during which Edouard Dujardin, in an article published by the *Revue Independante* on "Cloisonnism in Emile Bernard and Gauguin", established a relationship between Japanese art, Primitivism and Symbolism. Seven hundred prints were exhibited at the Académie des Beaux-Arts in 1890 that fired the imagination of the young *Nabi* painters and established the definitive triumph of Far-Eastern models. For the next decade, the Japanese influence was completely assimilated by western sensibility.

Japonisme first of all established itself in the field of the decorative arts, and also played an important part in the evolution of painting, not to mention the changing nature of exoticism.

Decorative Arts

With *Japonisme,* the "horror vacui" of eclectism made way for a real love of emptiness : the expressive autonomy of the surface was rediscovered. A potter like Carriès fashioned his work with his hands, allowing the baking to determine the enamel runs along on the outside of the stoneware. In the same way, Gallé integrated "the imperfections of creation", such as air bubbles, into his secret discourse of the decorative theme.

Around 1858, **Bracquemond** was among the first artists to discover Hokusai's famous collection of prints, *Manga.* More than the generally stated "influence" upon his work, he found in Japonisme an element to justify his prior studies in the field of engraving : a rising of parallel planes, the juxtaposition of multiple perspectives, unusual framing, or the placing of an isolated motif against a monochromatic background : a coherent research which coincided with that offered by the prints.

The bestiary ornamenting the series of plates in the **Service Rousseau** (1866, *cat. 116*) were also taken from numerous earlier sketches and aquatints, devoted to flora and fauna. Ducks in flight, water hens, lapwings, quail, tortoise and carp are to be found in Bracquemond's work from the early 1850's on. But the intention of the stylized forms, their isolation against the ground, the aquatic plants, the play of texture and atmosphere (a carp sliding upon the same white ground as that of a bee), elicit the subtle dialectic between occupied and unoccupied space that is the secret of Japanese Art. E. Chesneau stated, " Braquemond borrowed from the Japanese artists a liberty in the disposition of his motifs, not usually to be found in French decor; that is to say, the arbitrary displacement of focal points, the rupture of symmetry and of the proper balance of mass, the absolute usage of what I call asymmetry, the intelligent manner of placing an image at any point in the circle, since we are here dealing with plates, an ability to look beyond the geometric divisions of any given ornament, a flower petal, an insect, a large even

Cat. 117
Rousseau: Vase with Fish Ornament

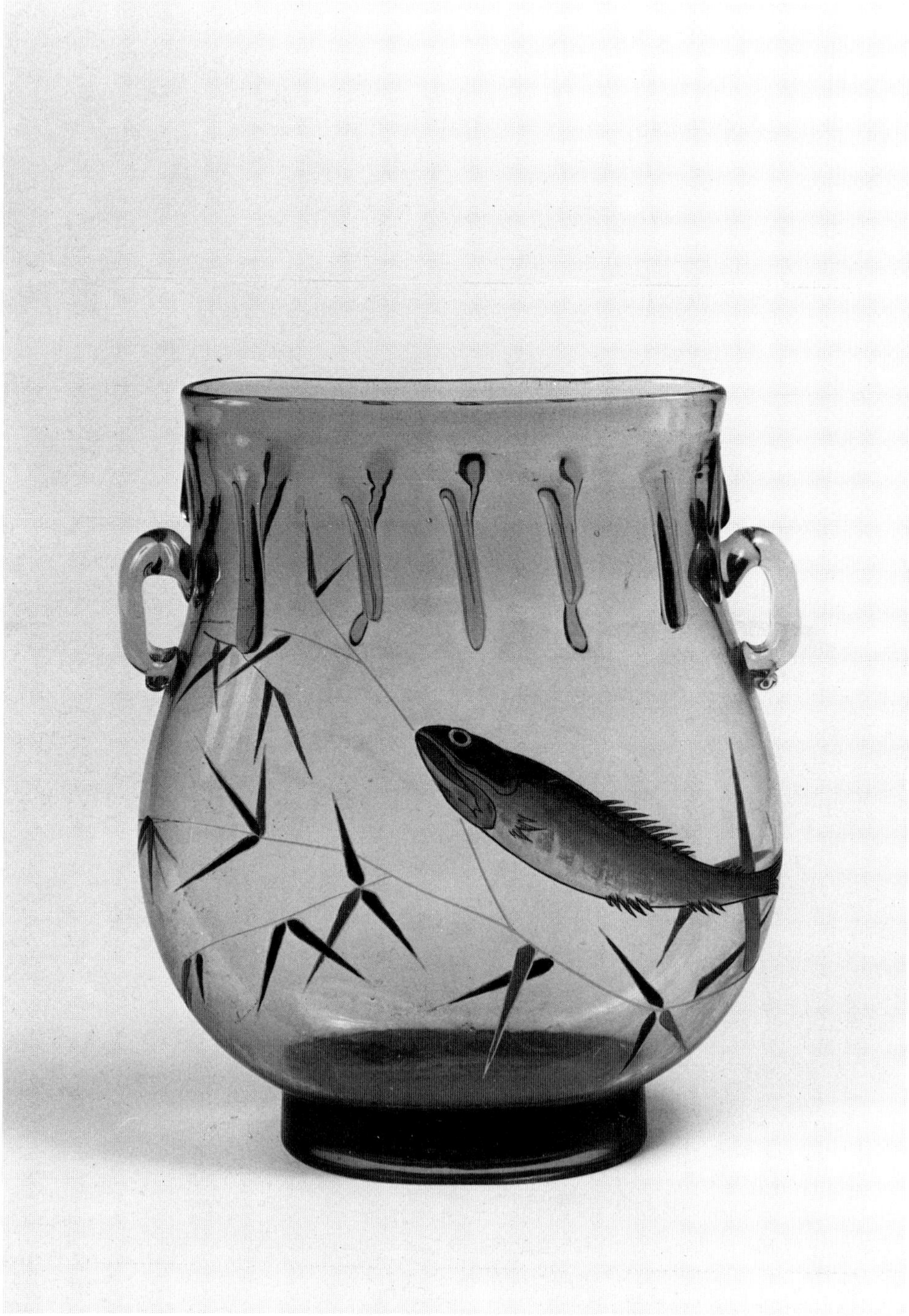

Cat. 116
Braquemond: Rousseau Table Service

Cat. 121
Godwin: Hanging
Display Cabinet

picturesque splotch (...) he borrowed their way of summary relief by flat tints which give an idea of the object without aiming at a trompe-l'œil effect (...)."

In architecture, the Japanese influence was not greatly felt before Wright and Mackintosh, the resistance of eclecticism being rather strong. This was also true in home furnishings : to have adapted the Japanese style would have meant a complete change of habit, one that only a true enthusiast, such as Whistler, was ready to adopt ; the borrowings in this realm remained somewhat superficial.

The case of the Englishman **Godwin** deserves special attention. He started buying Japanese objects in 1862 and papered his home with Japanese prints. His first pieces of furniture in the japanese style, along with the wall paper, textiles, and ceramic tiles were taken from original Japanese models.

The different types of furniture published in William Watt's *Art Furniture Catalogue* of 1877 are qualified as " Anglo-Japanese ". The massive volume of these mahogany pieces situates them firmly in the Victorian eclectic ; however, their decoration tended to become geometrical and airy despite a profuseness where exotism found refuge. With great elegance, the **bookcase** *(cat. 121)* unites all that Godwin retained from Japanese art in an exemplary manner : lightness of construction, total absence of ornamentation, a pre-eminence of right angles and a pronounced asymmetry.

Émile Gallé, born in Lorraine, animated every object with his pantheistic faith, borrowing his particular rhythms from the melody and poetry of

Cat. 120
Gallé : Coupe with Frog Ornament

Cat. 118
Gallé: Scent Bottle

Baudelaire, and above all, Verlaine. He retained from the Japanese a passionate contemplation of nature, by means of a stylization that conserved the essence of the object represented intact, while giving relief to the composition through a more moderate use of ornamentation.

It was in his earlier works that Gallé seemed to be under the direct influence of Japanese decorative arts, which he would sometimes content himself with merely reproducing. Three glass objects, **a scent bottle, a festooned vase, and a coupe** *(cats. 118, 119, 120),* reveal his emancipation from his earlier period (1880-84). His research into color, using injections of cobalt oxide, led to the creation of the opalescent saphire blue glass baptized *Clair de lune,* or *Moonlight Glass.* Gallé, a magician who created form, was an inspired chemist as well.

The marsh flowers, lotus leaves and poppies that ornament these objects float in an airy and acqueous element, where frogs and praying mantis congregate, forming an entomological carousel of disconcerting mobility.

Cat. 119
Gallé: Vase with Festooned Neck

Cat. 122
Michel: Vase

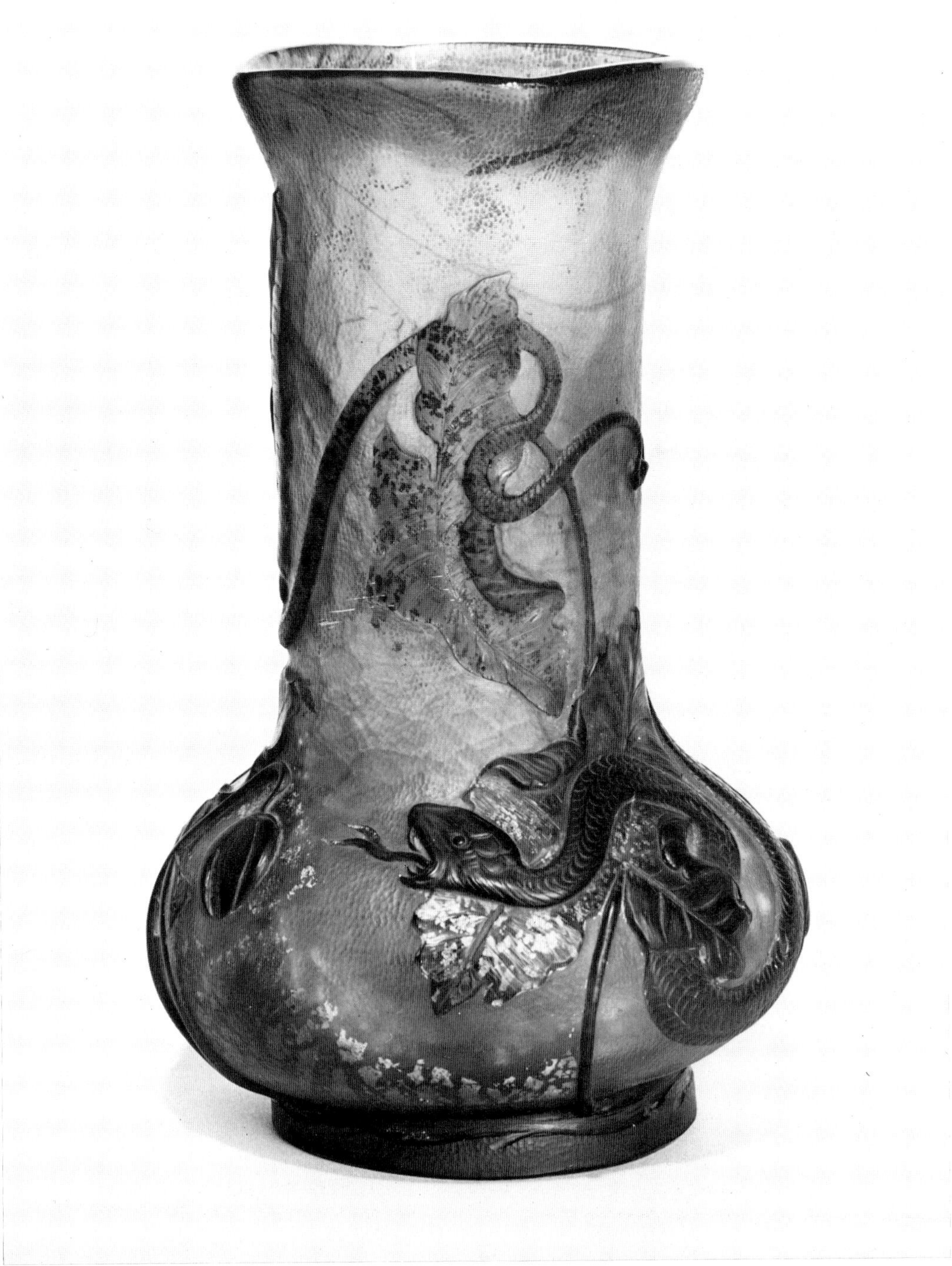

Other aspects of aquatic bestiary can be found in a vase of **Eugène Rousseau** *(cat. 117),* as well as in the rather delicate **vase by Eugène Michel,** *(cat. 122),* Rousseau's former associate.

Abandoning an exact imitation of Japanese decorative arts, Gallé remained totally faithful to his conception of nature and his work after 1890 seems to present a completely mastered art form. These vases onto which imperceptible movements of material have been melted, and whose surfaces are covered with the most precious tints, induced by copper, sulphur, silver, thallium or iridium, imprison splashes of color where the effects are burned into the surface by oxydation. These were the works admired by the Symbolists Henri Régnier and Robert de Montesquiou, as well as Proust, who on seeing them recounted:

" A vase by Gallé, saturated with fawn colored glitter,
Yawning like an orchid ;
Another streaked with mauve twilights. "

Painting

It is not known exactly when **Monet** first encountered Japanese art. The influence is not perceptible before the 1870's, the height of Impressionism; Whistler's *Princess du Pays de Porcelaine (fig. 111)* was painted in 1864.

The first Japanese quotations in Monet's work date from 1871 in *La Meditation, Mrs. Monet on the sofa,* with a fan posed upon the mantlepiece and the clearly cut silhouette of Camille Monet's wife, who is shown again in *La Japonaise* (1876, *fig. 112*), this time attired in a kimono. Fans fill the background, dangling in the air like so many trophies.

Fig. 111
Whistler: La Princesse du pays de Porcelaine (1864)

Fig. 112
Monet: La Japonaise (1876)

From this point forward a specific Japanese atmosphere, linked to nature by a discrete filter, determined Monet's works up until *The Pond of Water-lilies* at Giverny. A study of the *Thirty Six Views of Mount Fuji* by Hokusai may have inspired him in the variations on a single motif with modifications of light and atmosphere that intervene in his series of haystacks and cathedrals. Above all, he allowed himself to be progressively receptive to a Sino-Japanese pantheism of which his meditative *Nympheas* were to be the highest expression.

The sea painted in Brittany in 1886 also reveals a movement towards working in *series*. He wrote of his first sensations to his friend the painter Caillebotte : " I am in a countryside that is superbly savage, piles of incredible rocks and a sea of extraordinary color. I am completely overwhelmed. Having quite a time of it because I am used to painting the Channel where I had my little routine ; but the Ocean is really quite something else. "

His research into fuller and more severe motifs reveal a nature that is more resistant to human intervention. It is unsettling in his **Rocks of Belle-Ile,** *(cat. 109),* to see to what extent he approached photographic reality and how he also stylized the isolated elements in order to assert a synthetic vision of realism that Gauguin, Bernard, and Sérusier would later emulate in their own Breton works.

In Monet one finds a very subtle manifestation of Japonisme, illustrated here by his selection of several motifs from Suzuki Harunobu. Essential elements of this Japanese vision are the plunging perspectives and the high horizons. Monet is never simply an imitator. He succeeds both in rendering the extraordinary atmospheric glimmer of the Savage Coast, and in conserving the metaphysical depth of confrontation between sea and rock. Without going as far as the arabesque, he evokes the encounter of a pulsating and penetrating marine *yin* and *yang*. — perhaps Monet confused the whole Far East in one similar spiritual instability.

As far as the framing of compositions was concerned, **Degas** proved to be quite influenced by Japanese prints which he observed in the homes of Burty,

Fig. 113
Kiyonaga : Women bathing (c. 1780)

Cat. 109
Monet: Rocks in the Sea at Belle Ile

Duret, Alexis and Henri Rouart. He himself was a collector, although he did not go to the extremes of using a Japanese brush and *sumi* ink, or wear a kimono as was the case with Toulouse-Lautrec. He owned at least forty xylographies by Hokusai and two precious triptychs by Utamaro. *Manga* is the most frequent citation especially in his women bathing or combing their hair. His best-known paintings and pastels often reflect a personal way of organizing space that is similar to that of the *ukiyo-e* prints. His women ironing are often silhouettes against a pale background. The protagonists in *The Absinthe Drinkers* (1876), are off center ; *The Cotton Merchant's Office, New Orleans* (1873), *Diego Martelli* (1879) and *The Tub* (1886), are seen from above, whereas *Miss Lala au Cirque Fernando* (1879, *fig. 115*) is seen from below.

Fig. 114
Utamaro : Couple (A komuso with a lady) (c. 1790)

Continuing his steadfast refusal to emphasize the human figures, he shows them from behind, as in the engraving of his American painter friend **Mary Cassatt at the Louvre,** *(cat. 113)* standing in front of Etruscan tombs with a velvet-like elegance that recalls works from the Edo period.

Van Gogh was an avid reader of *Le Japon Artistique* and may have been inspired by a print by Harunobu (*A Young Girl Painting Flowers,* which appeared in the July 1888 issue) for his portraits of Madame Ginoux, **L'Arlésienne** *(cat. 112),* the proprietor of the railway Station café that he frequented with his friend Gauguin. In a letter to his brother Théo he exalted, " I have at long last found an Arlesienne, a figure thrown together in an hour with a pale lemon background, a grey face, dressed in black, black and black, that is to say a raw Prussian blue. "

Fig. 115
Degas : Miss Lala at the Fernando Circus (1879)

The edges of the somber mass are violenty cut, silhouetted against a monochromatic background in which the thick paint substance appears sculpted by the brush. The fervour of his touch does not prevent him from expressing the serene Madame Ginoux with sensitivity. Nevertheless, in this work he exhibits a tendancy towards abstract fullness paying tribute to the synthetization preached by Gauguin.

With the *Nabi* painters, a second generation of Japonisme developed. The first acquisitions from Japan had already been assimilated, and research now embarked on the progressive elimination of volume and the triumph of the continuous line. It seemed that the new comprehension of Japanese art aimed at deeper fulfillment.

The restoration of atmospheric verity in landscape, the Impressionist's *open window to the world,* seemed outdated to the Nabi who represented a particular moment in the history of painting on the fringes of Symbolism. For them, unlike Moreau or Redon, it was not a question of abolishing nature so as to activate a supernatural platonic universe, but of stimulating its meaning, by removing the proper value from objects and transforming them into signs, into the " letters of an immense alphabet " (Albert Aurier).

The new perspectives for twentieth century art that derived from the formal observations of the Nabis are well known. Maurice Denis, in a statement that foreshadowed the principles of Cubism and Abstraction claimed " to remember

Cat. 112
Van Gogh : L'Arlésienne

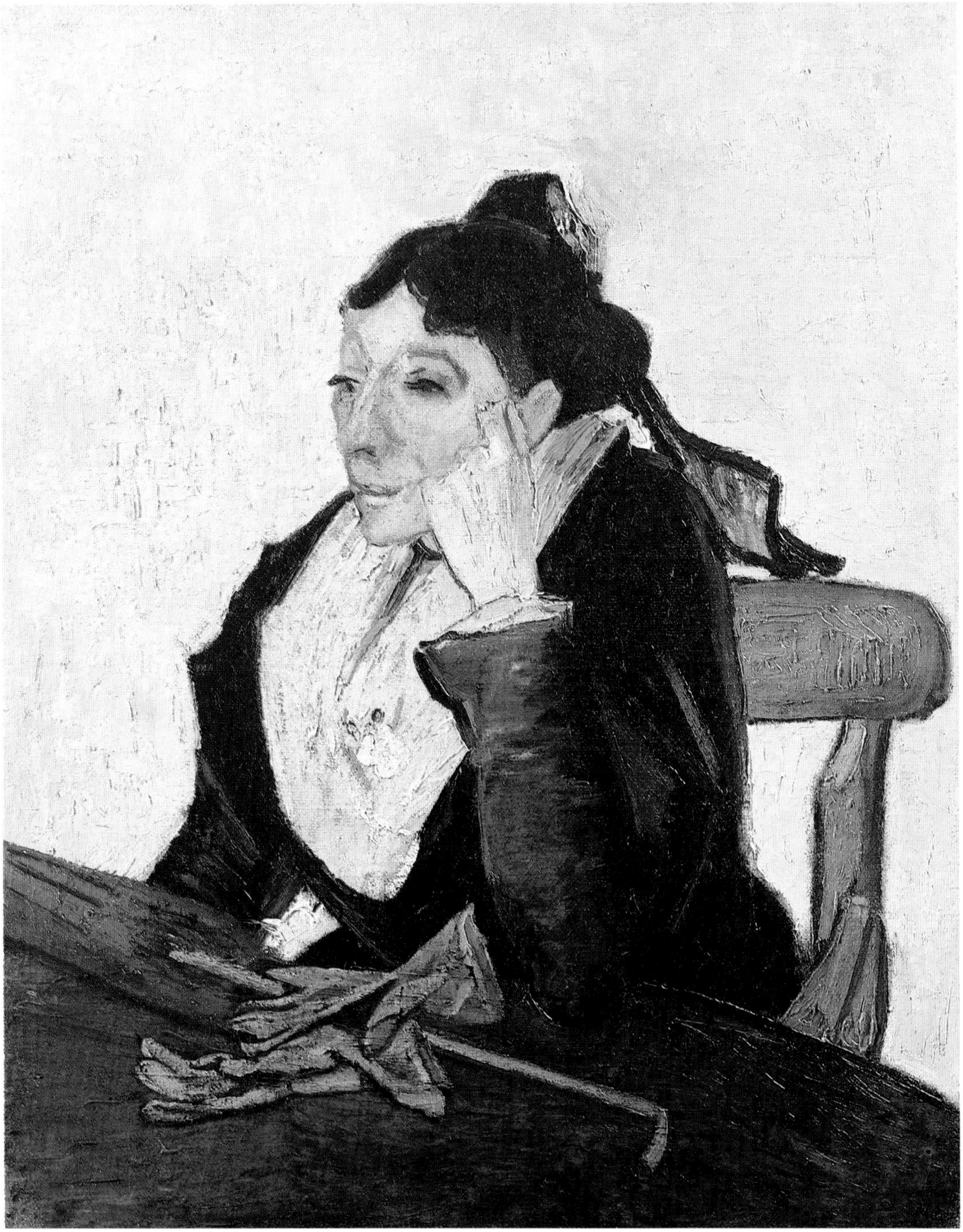

Cat. 107
Bonnard: The Croquet Game

that a painting, before being a battle horse, a naked woman, or some other anecdote, is essentially a flat surface covered with colors assembled in a certain order."

However, even in their most daring works, Maurice Denis, Sérusier, Lacombe or Verkade had no intention of radicalizing the formula : the arabesque and assertive archaism intervened with the ensemble of fixed rules. Rarely did their art depart from its position, rarely did it abandon its aspiration to be an access to a superior truth.

Pierre Bonnard, who his friends referred to as the *Japonard* Nabi, was not satisfied with random adaptations from the *ukiyo-e* colored prints. He understood that, in spite of appearances, Japanese art had its proper weight and perspective. Consequently, an isolated female figure is seen against a monochrome background in the process of making a series of movements : her head turned in a different direction from her bust, itself contradicting the orientation of her legs, communicating both the contrast and the density of the figure in space. The depth of field is evoked, no longer by the ' Italian ' central linear perspective, but rather by opposed oblique directions.

The Dressing-gown (1892, *fig. 116*) which develops lengthwise as a *Kakemono,* depicts a woman seen from the rear ; the vaguely sketched features of her lost profile cancel out her individuality ; the interest is entirely sustained by the sumptuous decoration of her clothing. Thus, the female-Sphinx of Symbolism retains its emblematic hold, only to become a mannequin, a luxurious playing card, who confers an unsuspected independance to the decorative scheme.

Fig. 116
Bonnard : The Dressing-gown (1892)

The masterpiece of Bonnard's Japanese period is, without a doubt, **The Croquet Game** *(cat. 107)* where elements that already existed are evoked in a family afternoon outing, super-imposed and seen together for the first time. At first glance we recognize the female figures and the dog in the center of the painting, slightly transposed and juxtaposed from *The Dressing-gown, The Woman with a Dog* and *Four Seasons.* If the men's faces are recognizable, the women's tend towards the emblematic.

The same poetry, which was similarly cherished by Vuillard, conceived clothing as a decorative surface with its obsessive network : speckled or checked surfaces that imprison the figures and place them against a background of equally vibrant colours.

The decoration dims the real space, depriving it of all illusionary depth. As in Hiroshighe's prints, the eye jumps from one plane to an other. The objects in the painting are not subject to the same perspective — the dog is seen more from above than the two women ; it is then up to the viewer to reconstruct the empty surface *as a penetrable space.*

The Downpour by Sérusier (1892, *cat. 110*) reveals a much more orthodox usage of the ' flat ' technique. The painter's palette is limited to opaque and earthy colors ; shades of terra-cotta and light somber greys. In a letter to his friend Verkade, the painter explained, " Three or four well chosen tints are enough, and they are expressive. The other colors only weaken the effect. "

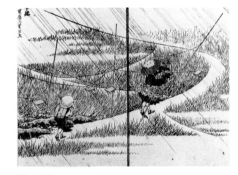

Fig. 117
Hokusai : Downpour on the Hill

Under the parallel lines of falling rain, the young Breton girl crossing the village square resembles a Japanese courtesan under her umbrella as she slips past an unbroken backdrop of flattened façades. The absence of thickness due to the partitioned colors, the impression of a collage of superimposed planes, render this painting even more radical than Bonnard's proceeding work. No vibration troubles the muffled space crossed by the melancholic and exiled geisha.

Like Gauguin, Sérusier knew how to communicate emotion with a certain fatalism allied to a secret sense of mystery, which makes Brittany the "land of prayers." A tendancy towards the monumental that he derived from both Giotto and Cimabue transforms this simple day's outing in the village of Huelgoat into a ritual ceremony and anticipates the majesty of his later works, with the pure geometry of the "Holy Measures" that he was later to preach.

The Japanese influences in **Maurice Denis** interact artfully with those of the Trecento (Italian 14th century). The sinuous tracing of his transparent angels and virgins owe as much to the contours of the *ukiyo-e* figures as they do to the apparitions of Beato Angelico. From these two sources derive the diaphanous bodies organized into faceless compact masses, subjugated to the group by a common contour as in *April* (1892) and in *Procession under the trees. (1893)*

Mother and child at the window (1901, *cat. 108*) admirably accomplishes the religious *mise en scène* of his own family life. The contours tightly encircling the flattened volumes evoke the linear perspective of the Japanese print. The extremely pure profile of the mother, meanwhile, recalls certain Madonnas from the Quattrocento (15th century) by Pisanello, Uccello, and above all Frà Angelico whom Maurice Denis adored : " ... He penetrated the mysteries of the inner life, and restored a feeling of its poetry ; he reclothed them with the most beautiful forms, and gave them the attitudes of our souls before God."

The window which cuts the landscape brings to mind Filippo Lippi's *Madonna with child and two angels* (c.1465, Uffizzi, Florence) ; it is the *finestra d'Alberti* looking out on to another portion of the world. Here, a pale-green sea is agitated by reverbrating interlacing ideograms, illuminating the infant and mother from behind. At first glance the planes seem superimposed, but a veritable space rises from the hyperbolic mobility of the composition's framing, restoring the depth of field within the direction of the light.

Exoticism

A deep understanding of the Japanese visual order was a gift possessed by few artists. To say that Japan was fashionable primarily signified that it had become a stock of exotic images, a repertoire of interchangeable decorative accessories inside a totally conventional space. They produced the same kind of jarring effect

Cat. 108
Denis: Mother and Child at the Window

that Parnassian poetry accumulated; a poem like *The Samourai* by J.M. de Hérédia (1842-1905) naturally fonctions as an amusing catalogue of clichés:

"... This handsome warrior, attired with lamina and armor,
Under the bronze, silk and brilliant lacquer,
Resembles a giant black and vermilion shell fish."

Nothing is missing: the sound of the *biva* (flute), the tresseled bamboo, the saber, " the two feelers trembling in front of his helmet". When exoticism deals with haute-couture, then nothing is easier than to dress up belly-dancers as geishas.

The dangers of the anecdote hover over the work of **Alfred Stevens** *(cat. 111)*, the Belgian society painter adopted by Paris. Passionately keen on Japanese curiosities, he filled his genre scenes, sentimental diaries of Parisian beauties, with lacquer, fans, vases and kimonos. In **La Lettre de Rupture** (1867), he painted a woman with a broken heart in an extremely conventional manner, positioned next to a Japanese folding screen, ready to let the fatal letter fall to the floor.

At first glance, this appears to be a typical scene by this painter of sugary subjects, but a closer look reveals a tendancy towards stylization; the simplification of detail leads to a refusal to disperse emotion upon the many objects that surround her. Instead he concentrates on her distress, expressed through a slight inclination of her body that evokes the courtesans painted by Utamaro.

Stevens in this way clothes his unchanging theme with a superficial Japanese coloring. He reveals a certain sensibility to the profound significance of the art of the print.

Japonisme in the work of Tissot is somewhat comparable. His *Lady with an Umbrella, Mrs Newton* (1877, *fig. 118*), is a small masterpiece with its simplifica-

Fig. 118
Tissot: Lady with an umbrella, Mrs. Newton (1878)

tion of mass and total abstraction of the landscape. His cycle of *The Prodigal Son* (1882), in which the protagonist is found abandoning himself to the pleasures of a Japanese brothel with an entourage of geishas dancing for him under a subdued red light, brings us abruptly in to the world of **Pierre Loti's** novels.

With **Madame Chrysanthème** (1887), the author of *Aziyadé* (1879) and of *"Island Fishermen"* (1886) influenced a succession of serial novels and plays embroidering endlessly upon a pattern of easy-to-assemble images. For the general public these were the very essence of the Empire of the Rising Sun, the incessantly reversible story of a western officer and a *geisha* surrounded by the odds and ends necessary to create the Japanese atmosphere: *mousmé, djins,* lotus flowers, oblivion sought in *saki,* young girls with solemn masks, clouds over the Bay of Nagasaki. In the wake of Japonisme came the innumerable novelettes, serials, and operettas, like the celebrated *Mikado* by Sullivan (1885) even the Fenouillard family *(fig. 119,120)* is seen stranded in the Land of the Rising Sun where, after insulting the Emperor, Mr. Fenouillard attempts hari-kiri with his umbrella.

In opera it is most probably Saint-Saëns, lover of Eastern musical tradition, who inaugurated the genre with his comic-opera *The Yellow Princess* (1872), the story of a scientist who dreams about a Japanese print and is transported to Japan.

Through this oneiric division of the personality, the enchantement in Gastinel's **Dream** is also achieved. It was first performed at the Paris Opera in 1890. Derived from a Japanese legend, this tale relates the story of how the young Daita escapes the grasp of the ferocious Sakuma with the help of the goddess Inazami, who appears at the summit of a giant fan and carries the heroine behind its leaves into a dreamy universe amid tentacular vegetation. The relatively well-known **poster** by **Steinlen** *(cat-114)* shows the incredible mixture of tutus and kimonos used in the "fantastique" choreography.

The opera *Iris* by Mascagni (1896) appears much more ethnographic. Surrounding the unusable plot of the frail mousmé coveted by compassionless

Fig. 119
The Fenouillard Family in Japan (1895)

Fig. 119 bis
The Fenouillard Family in Japan

Fig. 120
Degas: Woman bathing (monotype)

sadists, the composer of *Cavalleria Rusticana* provides an abundance of " exact " details of a Japan that remains defiantly phantasmagoric : a *shozi* with screen and wings, instrumental effects, gong, and *femme-objet,* plus two interesting ideas- a small puppet show in the first act, and the dead Iris dialogue in the last act, when she addresses the floating spirits of her torturers.

With *Madame Butterfly* (1904), based on David Belasco's play, Puccini situated a hieratic tragedy in an entirely contemporary Japan where everything can be bought with dollars. Puccini didn't hesitate to confront what was to become the moral blemish of the twentieth century, the incomprehension between cultures and races. We are the spectators of a slow-motion death ritual, the sort of interior monologue of a young girl cut off from reality, nestled in her dreams.

The elements borrowed from Japanese music are extremely infrequent, limited to the pentatonic scale, unusual intervals, and solo interventions of " exotic " sounding musical instruments such as the oboe and the flute in the heart of a transparent and sumptuous orchestration. Only inspired musicians like Stravinski in his very ascetic *Poésies de la lyrique Japonaise* (1913), expressed the decorative shimmer, the tendancy towards stylization, the expressive synthesis, and the economy of means proper to Japanese Art.

Painting

Bonnard Pierre (1867-1947), French

107 *The Croquet Game,* 1892
(La Partie de Croquet)
Oil on canvas (130 × 162 cm)
Signed and dated upper left: *P Bonnard 1892* (PB interlaced)
Gift of Mr. Daniel Wildenstein, 1985
RF 1985-8

Denis Maurice (1870-1943), French

108 *Mother and Child at the Window,* 1901
(Maternité à la fenêtre)
Oil on canvas (70 × 46 cm)
Signed bottom right: MAUD (vertical monogram)
Bequest of Paul Jamot, 1941
RF 1941-42

Monet Claude (1840-1926), French

109 *Rocks in the Sea at Belle-Ile* (1886)
(Rochers de Belle-Ile)
Oil on canvas (64 × 81 cm)
Signed and dated bottom right: *Claude Monet, 86*
Bequest of Gustave Caillebotte, 1894
RF 2777

Sérusier Paul (1863-1927), French

110 *The Downpour,* 1893
(L'Averse)
Oil on canvas (73.5 × 60 cm)
Lent by Mlle Boutaric, entered the Museum upon her death in 1983
RF 1981-7

Stevens Alfred (1823-1906), Belgian

111 *The Parting Letter or The Japanese Screen,* 1867-1868
(La Lettre de Rupture)
Oil on canvas (74.5 × 54.5 cm)
Signed mid left: *A Stevens* (A and S interlaced)
Acquired in 1983
RF 1983-26

Van Gogh Vincent (1853-1890), Dutch

112 *L'Arlésienne (Madame Ginoux),* 1888
Oil on canvas (92.5 × 73.5 cm)
Unsigned
Gift of Mme R. de Rotschild, 1944, entered Museum in 1974
RF 1952-6

Etching

Degas Edgar (1834-1917), French

113 *Mary Cassatt at the Louvre*
(Mary Cassatt au Louvre)
Etching (34.3 × 26.8 cm)
RF 4046D

Poster

Steinlen Théophile-Alexandre (1859-1923), French

114 Poster for *Le Rêve* ("Dream") by Gastinel, 1890
(78.5 × 60 cm)
Paris, Musée de la Publicité

Book

Loti Pierre

115 *Madame Chrysanthème*
Paris, Calmann-Lévy, 1888
Illustrations by Rossi and Myrbach

Objets d'art

Bracquemond Félix (1833-1914), French

116 *Rousseau Table Service* (model created in 1866)
(6 Assiettes du Service Rousseau)
Earthenware fabricated by Creil and Montereau (diameter 25.5 cm)
Acquired in 1982
OAO 667-679-682-691-692-695

Rousseau Eugène (1827-1891), French

117 *Vase with Fish Ornament* (1875-79)
     Enameled glass
     (25 × 18 cm)
     Acquired in 1984
     OAO 970

Gallé Émile (1846-1904), French

118 *Scent Bottle*
     Enameled and gilded glass
     (14.8 × 9.5 cm)
     Signed under the base: *Émile Gallé from Nancy /
     comp. / E.G.* with the Lorraine Cross / *registered*
     Acquired in 1981
     OAO 527

119 *Vase with Festooned Neck,* circa 1880-1884
     Frosted and enameled glass
     (25.3 × 19.9 × 15.8 cm)
     Signed under base: *E. Gallé / of Nancy / registered*
     Acquired in 1981
     OAO 529

120 *Coupe with Frog Ornament*
     Enameled glass
     (6 × 25 cm)
     OAO 891

Godwin Edward William (1833-1886), English

121 *Hanging Display Cabinet,* circa 1877
     (Étagère)
     Mahogany and glass (132 × 69.5 × 23.5 cm)
     Acquired in 1981
     OAO 578

Michel Eugène (1848-0000)

122 *Vase*(c. 1900)
     (diameter 30.4 cm)
     Acquired in 1984
     OAO 977

Landscapes

Landscape painting during the nineteenth century particularly confirmed its claim to nobility at a time when the Academy considered it as an inferior genre. Long before the Impressionists used the countryside as a priviledged laboratory for their investigations into optical sensation, artists like Alexander Cozens and Francis Towne had already faced the challenge of mountains. With Claude Lorrain as their model, numerous French painters depicted the Roman countryside as the archetype of an ideal nature : Géricault, Valenciennes and Corot added to the views of Rome and its surroundings where ruins stood as testimony to the futile efforts of the human will. Employing fewer historical references, the Englishmen Bonington and Constable were the true initiators of a landscape painting where the picture became a rendering of pure sensation without resorting to evocations of the traditional dialectic between the present and eternal.

For all, it nevertheless meant a transformation of nature perceived as a symbolic landscape of the inner-soul; man concealed by nature served as a dimensional unit of this painting, but mainly constituted its spiritual scale: his presence, often reduced to a fugitive notation, measured his boundless solitude confronted with the elements and bore witness to his resulting distress.

Théodore Rousseau's work can be situated between the Dutch and Constable. A perpetual wanderer over the French countryside, he and his friends of the Barbizon School (Diaz, Millet, and Daubigny) defined the major characteristics of the pre-Impressionist landscape. His **Pathway in the Forest of the Isle-Adam** *(cat. 11)* was still slightly determined by Romanticism with the lush vegetation that suffocates the foreground, while a soft golden light glows in a more open and pastoral middleground in bluish and rose tones which, as they dim, reveal an infinity swallowed by the opening in the trees.

Compared to this relatively humanistic and expansive conception, the Impressionist landscape offered a more pacified version of nature, one that was more domesticated and ordered by reason, or rather by industrial progress. The nature presented by the Impressionists, close to the urban centers, rejected the Romantic sublime and instead chose the calm waters of the canals, the metallic bridges which crossed over them, or even the railroads which scratched the countryside with their monotonous markings. Attempting to capture the illusive moment rather than achieve an immersion in nature, the Impressionist landscape established a sharp distance between the painter and the reality he depicted.

With Post-Impressionism the means of pictorial autonomy were accentuated, whereas the landscape was once again felt as the "impassioned equivalent of an achieved sensation" (Maurice Denis). It was with a small landscape, the *Bois d'Amour* (1888) by Sérusier (*Talisman* for the Nabis), that painting achieved its independence from nature through the use of pure partitioned color.

The Roman Burial Ground of Arles *(cat. 6)* painted by Gauguin a few months later is in some ways his *Talisman,* more finished, though perhaps less magical. The melancholic Arlesian walk, with tombs on either side, vibrates with the chromatic excesses of autumn. The eye first focuses upon the three women

Cat. 11
Rousseau: Pathway in the Forest of the Isle Adam

Cat. 6
Gauguin: The Roman Burial Grounds at Arles

Cat. 19a
Emerson: Marsh Leaves (The Waking River)

Cat. 19b
Emerson: Marsh Leaves (Corner of a Farmyard)

Cat. 21
Fockedey: Pavilion in a Park

dressed in traditional costume and then moves on to the romanesque ruins in the background ; but the emotions are mainly sollicitated by the general conflagration of the nature with its patches of orange and carmine evaporating in the cold blue of the sky. Announcing the agressivity of the Fauves, *The Burial Grounds* is no less solidly constructed with its vanishing point which raises the horizon line, an essential mark of the Post-Impressionist landscape.

At the same time, the English photographer, **Henry Emerson** seemed, in his own manner, equally sensitive to the revival of centering to which he was perhaps drawn by the Japanese model. His **Marsh Leaves** *(cat. 19)* constitute a point of equilibrium between the study of reality without pictorialist compromise and the temptation toward a more sophisticated organization of the image. His marshy landscapes, softened by the fog, achieve pure stylization without any manipulation during the developing or printing. We can evoke a true English tradition of the stylized photographic landscape if we consider the emaciated trees of George Shaw (1818-1904) or the compositions of **Fockedey** such as the **Pavilion in the Park** *(cat. 21)* which disturbs the viewer through simplification of mass.

Cat. 12
Sisley: Snow in Louveciennes

Snow covered landscapes constitute one of the most difficult excercises in style, as much by their consequential subduing of values as by the danger of standardizing color. **Claude Monet** appears to have toyed with these difficulties in his **Magpie** (1868, *cat. 9),* where he gives life to the subtlest iridescence in the white spectrum : the winter sun on the immaculate carpet of snow reveals bluish and pearl rose tones, whereas the shade of the fence creates an intermediate zone where pale greys dominate. Against its will, the Magpie is the sole sign of life in this scene completely encompassed by a cotton silence.

The Snow in Louveciennes by Sisley (1878, *cat. 12),* whose palette ranges from pearl grey to hints of sea green, is somewhat gloomy, if not completely desolate. In this severely structured composition, the vanishing points cross upon the solitary silhouette. The crystalline dazzle of the Magpie has here made way for a sort of empire of apathy. A **daguerrotype by Hossard** (1843) had already partially attained this sad and paralyzed atmosphere with its **Quays of Paris** *(cat. 22)* numbed by snow and ice.

· Seascapes are a genre which give a better idea of what is uncountable and immense. Before, the battle scenes on the high-seas painted by the Dutch were more often than not a mere pretext to let the sea element triumph. In his *Harmony in Blue and Silver : Trouville* (1865), Whistler translated the rhythms of the sea in totally dematerialized terms. The silhouette of Courbet upon the shore, more than

Cat. 22
Hossard : Paris Quays in the Snow

212

Cat. 8
Mesdag: Setting Sun

a simple challenge to eternity, appears as an attempt to dissolve into the very elements that the painting temporarily unifies.

Far from these cerebral heights, **Hendrik Mesdag** *(cat. 8)* painted relatively traditional seascapes. Here a setting sun diffuses its golden light over two-thirds of the composition while a few sailing boats attempt to disturb the free play of the bronze crests of the waves.

Compared to this prudent confirmation of tradition, any Neo-Impressionist seascape shows a veritable civilization gap. Seurat organizes his views of the sea at Grandcamp into skillful geometrics where the division of the paint atomizes the slightest iridescence, and Cross, in his *Golden Isles (fig. 121)* pulverizes reality into a rain of bluish ashes.

Because of his profound attachment to traditional perspective, **Théo Van Rysselberghe** remained the most reluctant of the Neo-Impressionists to geometrize form, the indespensible corollary of Divisionism. Nevertheless, in **Sailboats in the Estuary** the spectacle of the sea offered him the opportunity to radically stylize the elements and accentuate the principles of framing borrowed from the Japanese print. The space occupied by the sea is different to that in traditional seascapes (two-thirds instead of the usual one-third). The changing signs in the sky seem to be destined for dissolution in a mauve agony where the horizon line disappears and the faint strips of land, lit from behind, are dominated by dark contrasts of indigo and orange.

Through this rapid evolution, we can see that landscape painting, despite its apparent "eternal rules", has altered as much as the still-life or the portrait towards the flat surface, thus acquiring a total autonomy in regards to nature, to become one of the best measures of a confirmed modernity.

Fig. 121
Cross: Golden Islands (1893)

Cat. 14
Van Rysselberghe: Sailboats in the Estuary

Paintings

Gauguin Paul (1848-1903), French

6 *The Roman Burial Grounds at Arles*
(Les Alyscamps, Arles)
Oil on canvas (91.5 × 72.5 cm)
Signed and dated bottom left : *P. Gauguin, 88*
Gift of the Countess Vitali, 1923
RF 1938-47

Mesdag Hendrik (1831-1915), Dutch

8 *Setting Sun* (1887 Salon)
(Soleil couchant)
Oil on canvas (140 × 180 cm)
RF 497

Monet Claude (1840-1926), French

9 *The Magpie* (La Pie) 1868
Oil on canvas (89 × 130 cm)
Signed bottom right : *Claude Monet*
Acquired in 1984
RF 1984-164

Rousseau Théodore (1812-1867), French

11 *Pathway in the Forest of the Isle-Adam,* 1849
(Une Avenue, forêt de l'Isle-Adam)
Oil on canvas (101 × 82 cm)
Signed and dated bottom left : *Th. Rousseau, 1849*
Chauchard Bequest, 1906
RF 1882

Sisley Alfred (1839-1899), English-French

12 *Snow in Louveciennes,* 1878
(Neige à Louveciennes)
Oil on canvas (61 × 50.5 cm)
Signed and dated bottom right : *Sisley, 78*
Camondo Bequest, 1911
RF 2022

Van Rysselberghe Théo (1862-1926), Belgian

14 *Sailboats in the Estuary,* 1893
(Voiliers et Estuaire)
Oil on canvas (50 × 61 cm)
Signed bottom right : *VR*
Acquired in 1982
RF 1982-16

Photographs

Emerson Peter-Henry (1856-1936), English

19a *Marsh Leaves : The Waking River*
(6.5 × 9.5 cm)

19b *Marsh Leaves : Corner of a Farmyard*
(9.7 × 12.7 cm)
photogravure
Acquired in 1979
PHO 1979-74 and 762

Fockedey Hippolyte (?-?), English

21 *Pavilion in a Parc,* 1853
(Pavillon dans un parc)
Negative paper (15.5 × 17.8 cm)
Acquired in 1983
PHO 1984-194

Hossard Professeur (?-?), French

22 *Paris Quays in the Snow,* 1843
(Quais de Paris sous la Neige)
Daguerreotype (7.5 × 10 cm)
Gift of the Kodak-Pathé Foundation, 1983
PHO 1983-65 (4)

Waltz

Far from the ball, in the damp park
Already flowering with lilac,
He held me in his arms.
How madly one loves at that timid age.

 During a triumphal evening
 In the park, far from the ball,
 He told me this blasphemy:
 "I love you".

 Then I went each evening,
 White in the dark wood,
 To see him again
 He, my hope, my supreme hope.

Far from the ball, in the damp park
How madly one loves at that timid age.

II

In the ardent waltz he carries you
Blond green-eyed fiancée:
He will die from your perverse look,
Me, I am already dead from his love.

 During a triumphal evening
 In the park, far from the ball
 He told me this blasphemy:
 "I love you".

 Never to see him again...
 At the moment all is black;
 To die this evening
 Is my hope, my supreme hope.

He carries me in the ardent waltz.
I am forgotten and dead.

Charles Cros *Le Collier de Griffes*
(The necklace of claws)

Cat. 123
Renoir: Dance in the Country

Cat. 124
Renoir: Dance in the City

Renoir Auguste (1841-1919), French

123 *Dance in the country*
(Danse à la campagne)
Oil on canvas (180 × 90)
Signed and dated bottom left : *Renoir.83.*
Acquired in 1979
RF 1979-64

124 *Dance in the city*
(Danse à la ville)
Oil on canvas (180 × 90)
Signed and dated bottom right : *Renoir.83.*
Acquired by state in lieu of state taxes in 1978
RF 1978-13

Sources for the Figures

Baltimore
  Walters Art Gallery (70, 72)
Boston
  Museum of Fine Arts (51)
Brest
  Musée municipal (7)
Detroit
  Institute of Fine Arts (56)
Florence
  Museo Nazionale (24)
  Uffizzi (18)
Gray
  Musée Baron Martin (118)
London
  British Museum   (109)
  National Gallery (81, 115)
  Tate Gallery (54, 77, 106)
  Victoria & Albert Museum (44, 99)
  Royal Photographic Soc. (73)
  Priv. Coll. (62)
Lyon
  Musée des Beaux-Arts (21)
Madrid
  Prado (20)
Manchester
  City Art Galleries (88)
Milan
  Galleria Civica d'Arte Moderna (89)
Moulins
  Musée des Beaux-Arts (71)
Munich
  Neue Pinakothek (57)
Nantes
  Musée des Beaux-Arts (23)

New York
  Brooklyn Museum (79)
  Museum of Modern Art (30)
Oxford
  Ashmolean Museum (53)
Paris
  Bibliothèque nationale, Cabinet des Estampes (2, 4, 13, 19, 29, 33, 36, 41, 59, 60, 69, 80, 104, 105, 114, 117)
  Bibliothèque de l'Opéra (43, 45, 49, 52, 55, 68)
  Musée du Louvre (16, 22, 27, 28, 63, 66, 75)
  Musée d'Orsay (1, 3, 5, 9, 10, 11, 12, 14, 15, 17, 34, 35, 40, 46, 47, 48, 58, 64, 65, 82, 86, 87, 90, 91, 92, 103, 116, 121)
  Musée d'Orsay Bibliothèque (25, 37, 38, 39, 84, 85, 95, 96, 97, 98, 107, 108, 119, 120)
  Centre de Recherche des Monuments Historiques (76, 94)
Rochester, N. Y.
  George Eastman House (74, 83)
Rome
  Galleria Doria-Pamphilij (50)
Saint-Germain-en-Laye
  Musée du Prieuré (78)
Strasbourg
  Musée des Beaux-Arts (8)
Troyes
  Musée des Beaux-Arts (93)
Versailles
  Musée national du Château (26, 31)
Vienna
  Albertina (61)
  Österreichische Galerie (42)
  Priv. Coll. (102)
Washington
  National Gallery (6)
  Freer Art Gallery (110)

Photo credits

Designed by Bruno Pfäffli

Color engravings S.R.G., Paris

Set and printed in France by Imprimerie Blanchard